GATHER BY THE AVON

THE STRATFORD STORY PROJECT BOOK

GATHER BY THE AVON

THE STRATFORD STORY PROJECT BOOK

by
LINDSAY KROES

Cover design by Julien Hradecky.
Front cover photo: Stratford Perth Archives.

GATHER BY THE AVON.
ISBN 978-0-9920598-0-4
Copyright ©2013 Recollections Publications
Published by Recollections Publications
    1903 Perth Line 43
    New Hamburg, Ontario
    N3A 3Z5
    www.stratfordstoryproject.ca

Contents

Preface

In May 2013, I launched the Stratford Story Project. Part community history, part storytelling, the project aimed to collect and preserve the stories of Stratford residents, based on the firm belief that everybody has a story to tell. With digital recorder in hand, I set out to interview fifty seniors in the Stratford area. I began with the simple question, "Where were you born, and when?" From there, I was taken on fifty very different adventures through the memories of the individuals I interviewed. Then, I sat down to capture their stories on paper. This volume is the result.

As the title suggests, this book is a gathering—a gathering of stories, told by residents of Stratford and the surrounding area between the ages of 70 and 98. They appear in the book in no particular order. Selection of the participants arose organically with assistance from local retirement homes and seniors programs, as well as referrals from family and friends. Some of the individuals interviewed have lived in Stratford their whole lives, others have settled here only recently. All generously and graciously welcomed me into their homes and their past—and as you will discover, they each had a wonderful story to tell.

The inspiration for this project came from a very unique co-op job that I had last fall. For four months, I worked as a historical interpreter at Doon Heritage Village, a turn-of-the-century living history site which is part of the Waterloo Region Museum. Visiting the village is a bit like strolling through the past. Every building, from the general store to the farmhouse, is maintained exactly as it would have been in 1914.

It was my job to teach visitors and school groups about

life in the year 1914—but in some ways, I also lived it. Each morning, I donned a full-length skirt and a puffed-sleeve blouse, and tucked my hair beneath a straw hat as befitting a proper lady in the early twentieth century. On sunny mornings, you could find me in the backyard wrestling laundry through the wringer washer. On rainy afternoons, I might be in the parlour, bent over my knitting or squeezing music from the wheezy pump organ. I learned to fiddle with the coal oil lamp until the wick was set at the perfect height—enough to cast a flickering light without blackening the chimney entirely. As the days grew colder, I would coax a fire to life in the majestic black woodstove in the kitchen and mix up a batch of cookies (although I admit that I never mastered the art of baking without an oven thermometer).

Me, on the right, in full 1914 attire.

Somewhere in those four months, I was struck with a realization. The lifestyle I was experiencing and teaching others about at Doon felt incredibly novel and distant to me—but to many seniors, it is well within their memory. Of course, very few people remain who lived in 1914 (indeed, the oldest individual interviewed for this book was born one year later, in 1915). However, the tasks I mentioned above were routine parts of many people's childhoods.

This sentiment was confirmed by elderly visitors to the site, who would frequently recognize the wall-mounted telephone, the big tin washbasin, the hand-crank gramophone, and other artifacts from their own experience. Often these pieces would spark reminiscences, and they would launch into a story of Saturday night baths in front of the stove or kitchen dances on summer evenings. Their stories were entertaining and surprising as well as rich with social history.

There is something special about stories. In some ways, they are the legacy we leave and the vessel through which our wisdom can be passed on. They teach us about history from a completely different perspective than a textbook—a perspective which captures the quirks of human nature and demonstrates the myriad of ways in which individuals are shaped by grand historical events. They help us to see the extraordinary in the ordinary. My experience at Doon opened my eyes to the wealth of stories that seniors have to share and the value in recording them.

When I returned to my English and history studies at the University of Waterloo, I decided to undertake the Stratford Story Project during my summer co-op term. Stratford is a city with a vibrant and varied past. During the Depression years, it was the site of one of the most prominent general strikes in Canadian history, a conflict so intense that the army was summoned to dispel strikers. The city was actively involved in the production of war materials during the Second World War, while also housing both the Perth Regiment and a battalion of Dutch soldiers over the course of the war. In the years since, Stratford has transformed from a manufacturing hub centred around the Canadian National Railway and the furniture factories, to a sophisticated, world-renowned cultural attraction—all without losing its small-town charm. I felt sure, in the midst of all this history, there were some wonderful stories to uncover.

I was not mistaken.

I would like to offer my heartfelt thanks to the individuals who shared their stories for this book. It was my privilege to get to know each of them. Though many insisted that their stories were nothing special, I found that the opposite was true. On a personal level, this project has been illuminating, challenging, and rewarding. I have learned a lot, not only about the city in which I grew up but also about life in general—about embracing change, finding joy in each day, and maintaining lifelong relationships.

I hope you enjoy these stories as I have.

The Generosity of Neighbours
Marj Gibson

The young girl clutched her ticket as she crossed Ontario Street and made her way to the parking lot of Avalon Fabrics. Her mother had sent her on an important errand, and she was determined to be equal to the task. A small group was already gathered in the lot, each with their own tickets. They were chatting as they waited in the ever-growing line. The girl took her place at the end, greeting her neighbours as she did. Finally, a large truck pulled up and the back doors opened. The stern relief agent began to hand out loaves of bread, one for each person. When she reached the front, the girl exchanged her ticket for a fresh loaf. Its warm smell wafted through the air as she tucked it under her arm and turned her steps towards home.

Marj Gibson proudly counts herself as an "East Ender"—she was raised in the midst of Stratford's booming manufacturing sector, close enough that the whistles from the nearby Preston-Noelting Furniture Factory punctuated her childhood. She describes growing up in Stratford as "freedom." Everything they needed was within walking distance, and she spent many happy hours playing with the neighbourhood children. In the summer, they would keep one ear cocked for the ice cream vendor's bell as he toured up and down the streets. Doctors made house calls then, as did photographers. All of Marj's baby pictures were taken by a photographer who went door to door. Marj's mother was known

1

Marj as a baby.

as 'The Queen of King Street,' a testament to the strong community ties that the family held. During the tough days of the Great Depression, this close-knit community was especially crucial, as factory workers were hit hard by the economic troubles of the day.

Marj's father worked at Kroehler's Furniture Factory, which employed many people at that time in Stratford. His job was 'spitting tacks:' he would put a mouthful of tacks between his lips, then use them to affix upholstery to chesterfields with a magnetic hammer that grabbed the tacks one by one. At that time, workers were paid by piecework; they had a quota to meet each day, and if they didn't meet it, they would be charged. As the thirties wore on, the high quotas and low pay became especially onerous. Labour unrest began to stir, in Stratford and across the country, as workers felt they were being 'kept down.' This came to a head in Stratford with the arrival of the Worker's Unity League in 1933. The league began organizing local workers and soon a general strike had erupted across the city, beginning in September with the furniture factories and quickly spreading to food workers as well. Animosity between city officials and workers began to brew, which intensified when the mayor called in the militia to maintain order in the city.

This action only made matters worse, stoking resentment. Marj recalls riding with her father on a truck packed with other strikers. They drove up and down the streets of town, singing "the old grey mayor, he ain't what he used to be." One day she looked across the street to the Preston-Noelting Factory to see workers throwing radio cabinets out the windows. Her father was a mild-mannered, well-liked man, and he went over to try to settle the workers down. However, the month-long strike caused lasting divisions in the city. The mayor and most of the city council resigned following the incident and were replaced by a pro-labour city government.

Meanwhile, for East Enders like Marj, community was the key to survival during the Depression years. She was fortunate to have relatives on the farm, whose gardens supplied surplus produce for Marj's family meals. The local grocer was also an invaluable source of assistance. In Marj's neighbourhood, Pat Powell operated a little store nearby. Knowing who was trustworthy, Pat would sell goods on credit to many families. Frequently, Marj's mother would send her down the store with a note and a little bit of money to put against the bill, and she would return with the groceries for the evening meal. Doctors, too, allowed patients to pay on credit. Each week, Marj's mother put 25 cents towards her doctor's bill. The credit system was the only way that families could manage during rough times, and they were grateful for the small-town kindness that allowed it.

One Christmas in the thirties, money was awfully tight for Marj's family. They had moved several times during the Depression, each time to a smaller place where the rent was lower. The family was used to scrimping, saving, and mak-

Marj and her mother.

ing do with less, but that year there just didn't seem to be enough to make ends meet. On Christmas Eve, they opened their front door to find a basket waiting on their doorstep, sent by their church. It had extra food and fixings for the Christmas meal and a few small treats for under the Christmas tree. That thoughtful gift brought some extra Christmas cheer which the family truly appreciated. As soon as they were able, they returned the generosity, scraping together enough money to buy a doll to send to the church mission in Timmins.

Looking back on the Depression, it is not memories of the desperation and hardship of those years that emerge, but rather the benevolence of the community which offered help when it was needed, expecting nothing in return. The friendships formed during Marj's early years in the East End have remained with her for the rest of her life.

Nights in Nanaimo

Marie Strahm

It was her first night in Nanaimo, British Columbia, and Marie was terrified. She looked over to the bed where her son slumbered on, undisturbed by the shots that had just crashed through the still night. In the street below there was no movement. Abruptly, another round of shots broke the silence. They were coming from the harbour, and she feared it was the Japanese.

A few days ago, she had received word that her husband would be shipping out in a few weeks. She caught a train the next day, her suitcase in one hand, her two-year-old son in the other, and her ticket between her teeth. Undaunted by the distance, she was determined that her husband would spend his last weeks on Canadian land with his family. It had been a beautiful reunion at the train station. At the end of the evening, her husband returned to his army camp and she to her rented room, where she now sat alone as the shots reverberated through the night.

Suddenly, a noise on the street brought her back to the window. A car with a megaphone on the top was driving slowly by. Its message announced that there was a naval drill taking place in the harbour, nothing to be alarmed about.

The year that Marie Strahm was born, 1916, the April showers had been particularly rampant. On the way to her delivery on April 26, the doctor's car became stuck in a mud-

Baby Marie with her aunt.

hole on the rustic country road. Marie's father had to haul
the doctor out with a team of horses before his daughter's
birth. A few years later, the family moved into New Hamburg, where Marie attended school. The New Hamburg Continuation School went only to grade twelve, so for grade thirteen, she took the train into Kitchener every day. Since there
was no passenger train to take her home in the evenings, she
caught a ride on a freight train, often arriving as late as
eight o'clock. To pass the long hours at the train station, she
learned to play cards.

Several years after high school, Marie's sister set her up
on a blind date with a man named Earl—though everyone
called him 'Flanny.' "At first I thought he was stuffy," she
recalls. "But he kept calling, so I came around." After a
six-year courtship, they married in 1941. Since Flanny was a
mechanic, he had been recruited to repair the training planes

at the Air Force Base near Goderich, so they spent the first years of their marriage there. Sometimes he had to fly in the planes as a passenger, and he often got home for lunch looking rather shaken when the planes weren't quite flight-ready.

Eventually, Flanny was called up for active service. After a short stint in Peterborough, he was sent to Nanaimo, a harbour city on Vancouver Island. When he left, Marie moved with her baby son into New Hamburg. Their house was right around the block from her parents, but it had its drawbacks. The previous owner had kept chickens in the up-stairs bedroom, leaving a foul odour which pervaded the entire house for weeks. The spring brought a flood which put the basement completely underwater. Marie remembers walking downstairs to see the crock of apple butter that she stored in the fruit cellar bobbing in the water. She didn't live at the house for long before travelling out West to be with her husband.

The train trip with her nearly two-year-old son was a trying experience. They slept in the same bunk at night and spent the days watching the Canadian Prairies pass by their window. The bitter cold in Regina shocked her. She had planned to call her uncle from the train station, but the moment she stepped outside, the cold stole her breath so quickly that she changed her mind. She wrote a note from the warmth of her compartment and passed it to the conductor to call for her. Finally they arrived in Nanaimo, and she rented a room in an older woman's house.

Marie and her husband filled the few days they had left with many happy hours together. However, the day came all too soon for him to ship out. Marie accompanied several other wives to the train station, sharing tear-stained glances. They were standing on the platform when suddenly there was a kerfuffle at the door of the train. Six of the men were pulled off the train because they were needed in Nanaimo.

Marie and Flanny on their wedding day.

Marie could hardly believe her good fortune when Flanny was among them.

Marie and Flanny rented a converted garage to live in, while Flanny continued to work in the kitchen at the army base. So many wives had come to Nanaimo to be with their military husbands that there were hardly any men who took their meals at the camp anymore. Flanny would bring home some of the ample leftovers for their own dinner. The army chef was quite skillful, so they appreciated this very much.

On one occasion, after spending the evening downtown with friends, Marie and Flanny took the bus back to their house. They disembarked at the bus stop only to find themselves in complete darkness. All the windows were covered by black-out curtains as a precaution against bombing, and the streetlights had all been extinguished. They literally could not see where they were.

"Do you know how to get home?" Flanny asked.

"Sure," Marie said, with false confidence. She set off to lead the way—but instead led them straight into a ditch. They had a good laugh for a few minutes, before finding their bearings and turning towards home.

They spent the duration of the war in Nanaimo. On VJ Day (the day that the Japanese surrendered), Marie was awakened before dawn by the noise of the crowd, already creating a happy ruckus in the streets. There were people playing the metal spoons and long lines of human chains winding and circling downtown. Such a spontaneous and jubilant celebration Marie has never witnessed since.

After the celebrations quieted and the news sunk in, Marie and Flanny became anxious to return to their family back home. They came by train in December 1945, arriving in Toronto on Christmas Eve in the midst of a great blizzard. While they waited for the storm to abate, they bided their time in Eaton's Department Store. Their son—now nearly five—raced from one display to the next, his eyes wide as he surveyed all the toys. Exhausted from having spent the past few nights crammed into one bunk, it was all they could do to keep track of him in the crowded hubbub of last-minute shoppers.

Finally, at nine o'clock that evening, their train pulled into the New Hamburg station, where Marie's father was waiting for them. They were exhausted from their travels, but that Christmas Eve was a happy one for their whole family. The war was over, and they were all together again.

9

The Horse that was a Hero
Elmeda Martin Baker

Elmeda's eyelids grew heavy as the cutter-sleigh jolted forwards. Curled around the reins, her numb fingers shivered uncontrollably while the horse lunged through the drifts. The pull of sleep was pervasive, and her thoughts grew sluggish and confused.

Only hours earlier, she had been at school when rumours began to circulate about an impending blizzard. She called home to ask whether she ought to sleep over in Winterbourne, a small town northeast of Waterloo where the school was located. "If you leave now, I think you'll make it before the storm hits," her father told her. Elmeda and her horse set off for home under a blanket of grey clouds. They were halfway there when the cutter swung too sharply around a corner and toppled to the side, dumping Elmeda into a snow drift. She brushed herself off and righted the cutter, hurrying to be on her way again as the heavy snow started to fall. The trip normally took an hour and a half, but it seemed to drag on and on as the snow melted through Elmeda's coat and seeped onto her skin.

When she finally arrived at the farm, Elmeda was barely conscious. The horse hauled the cutter into the front yard, across the snow drifts, and onto the porch, right to the kitchen window. She nudged the frosted panes with her nose to get Elmeda's parents' attention. Within minutes, Elmeda was whisked inside, and the horse was led

10

to her warm barn stall—both of them safe from the storm.

Elmeda Martin Baker spent the first 21 years of her life on a farm north of Conestoga in Waterloo Township. She was born in 1919, an only child until she was eight, when the household welcomed a new baby brother to the family. After that, a baby arrived each year until there were six kids, so Elmeda was always called upon to help her mother. After she learned to sew, it became her responsibility to make all of her siblings' clothes with homemade patterns cut out of newspaper—blouses and pants for the boys and dresses for the girls.

Elmeda enjoyed school, but it was quite rare for students in her area to go to high school. Besides, her help was needed on the farm. "I always had a hankering after more learning," she recalls, and she kept her eyes open for opportunities. She hoped to attend Bible School in Kitchener, but her father couldn't afford to send any of the other children, so he didn't think it would be fair to send Elmeda. Undeterred, Elmeda heard about a Short Course that was being held in the nearby town of Winterbourne and resolved to attend.

The Short Course was a local form of continuing education which took place in the winter, when most farm youth had some time to spare. There were classes in animal husbandry, field husbandry, nursing, sewing, and cooking, and it cost 75 cents a month to attend. When she heard about the course, Elmeda hurried home to count her savings. As a child, her aunts and uncles would sometimes give her a dime as a gift when the family went visiting on Sunday afternoons. In addition, she had some money left over from the last fall fair which she hadn't used. Pooled together, she was able to come up with enough for tuition.

With that obstacle cleared, she still had to convince her father to allow her to go. He said, "If you are willing to hitch up the horse and cutter by yourself each morning and unhitch it each night, I am willing to let you go." He didn't think she would go to the trouble, but she did. Every morning, she bundled up against the bitter winds, hitched up the horse and drove to Winterbourne, arriving in time to begin classes at 8:30 a.m. Her horse, a sorrel mare named Jane, knew the way and carried her home safely each night, even through the winter's worst blizzard. Though she arrived home frostbitten and freezing cold, Elmeda was back in the cutter again the following Monday, on her way to school. When she graduated, she was Second Girl in her class. The First Girl in the class won a trip to Ottawa; Elmeda was less enamoured with her prize, which was a recipe file.

Afterwards, Elmeda continued to work on her family farm. During the yearly threshing one autumn, she was helping to fill the granary when her feet slipped on the kernels, and she fell, landing so hard on her stomach that her appendix ruptured. The pain was immediate and staggering. Her father didn't realize the extent of her injury so he instructed her to go herd the cows into another pasture. When she told him she could hardly walk, he said, "You'll be fine, just take the dog with you."

He felt terrible when they eventually realized what had happened, but it took some time to be diagnosed. Elmeda spent days on the couch, hoping that the stomach pain would subside on its own. Friends of the family offered the suggestion that she crawl down the stairs headfirst on her abdomen, which they thought might soothe her stomach. Of course, it made no difference. After a few months the pain lessened, but in its place a rash sprung up on her arms and face so Elmeda was finally taken to the doctor.

When the doctor took an X-ray, he could not find her appendix at all. It had burst and grown into the bowel in the intervening months. The situation was so severe that doctors were surprised she was still living. After surgery, she spent fourteen days in St. Mary's Hospital, which was staffed by nuns at the time. One afternoon, she was resting in her bed when a nun came in with a short broom to sweep out behind the radiators.

"I thought you might like to have your back scratched," the nun joked, sending Elmeda into peals of laughter. She laughed so hard that she broke open her stitches and had to spend another fourteen days in the hospital. Later, she was distressed to find out that the nun had been fired for the incident. Her surgery and extended stay added up to a doctor's bill of $200, an exorbitant sum that Elmeda's family simply did not have. As soon as she was well enough, Elmeda took a job in Elmira as a housekeeper for the town's wealthiest lady. Half of her weekly salary of $4 was put towards the doctor's bill. When the doctor found out she was paying her bill this way, he waived the rest of her fee. "It's paid for," he said and wouldn't hear anything else about it.

Elmeda on her wedding day.

13

After a couple of years, Elmeda moved out to a farm to keep house for a man and his ill mother. He was fourteen years older than she was, so at first she didn't give him a second look. One day, after she'd been working there for several years, he invited her to come along with him to Elmira where they had lunch in a restaurant. When they returned, he asked her if she would like to do it again sometime.

"As long as you pay for it," she replied innocently. After a few more dates, she caught on and began to grow very fond of him as well. Two years later, ninety guests filled her childhood home to celebrate their wedding ceremony.

After her marriage, Elmeda put her seamstress skills to work on bridal wear and later custom draperies. She and her husband raised two daughters in their home in Elmira. They retired to Greenwood Court in Stratford, and her husband passed away.

Years later, Elmeda met another special man who lived on her floor in the apartment building. She couldn't have been more surprised when he proposed, but she accepted. Their wedding in 2004 was a happy day for all Greenwood residents.

Elmeda and her husband on their wedding day.

Nights at the Crystal Palace
Shirley Pautler

*The steamy laundry room of the hospital was
filled with giggling girls. Each new item that they
pulled from the laundry sack provoked fresh peals
of laughter. Far from the drab bedsheets and gowns
that they were accustomed to seeing, today they
were charged with washing flouncy pantaloons,
colourful velvet vests, and glitzy blouses. The shoes,
curved at the end with a little bell suspended from
the tip, elicited the most mirth.*

*These clothes had been sent over earlier that
afternoon from the Festival Theatre, then a fledgling venue still operating out of a tent. Hutchisons,'
the laundromat which usually handled the cos-
tumes, had broken down, and they were desperate
for someone to take over the job. The girls muffled their laughter and got straight to the task.
Thanks to the quick work of the hospital laundry
girls, the actors donned fresh clean clothes for the
evening's Shakespearean production.*

Shirley Pautler was born in St. Marys, the eldest of ten
children. Growing up, there always seemed to be another
baby coming into the house, and Shirley was used to caring
for her younger siblings. Their home had no indoor plumb-
ing, so all the kids had 'Charlie pots' beneath their beds
which had to be carried each morning through the house
and the summer kitchen to the outhouse in the backyard—
that is until it was burned to the ground by pranksters one
Halloween.

Saturday was bath night. Shirley's mother would fill a big tub with warm water from the stove reservoir. In the warmth cast by the open oven door, the whole family would have their weekly bath from oldest to youngest. Then, Shirley's hair would be tied up in rags, which would be unravelled the next morning before church to reveal perfect ringlets. The next day the curls would be brushed out into waves, and for the rest of the week, she would wear her hair in pigtails.

Shirley at three years of age.

The family lived near the school, so Shirley and her siblings walked home each day for lunch. They knew it was time to hurry back to school when they heard "Knock, knock! Who's there? It's the Happy Gang!" from their radio. It was a popular show which always came on at one o'clock. Shirley loved school and hated to miss a single day because students were given a silver dollar for a year of perfect attendance.

Shirley, holding her baby sister and surrounded by siblings.

On July 1, 1949, Shirley's friend invited her to hitchhike into Stratford with her. She was determined to get a job at the Avon Crest Hospital, which was *the* place to work at the time. Obligingly, Shirley accompanied her to the interview with the stern head nurse, Minerva Snyder. Her friend was given a job as a ward aide. Then, Minerva turned to Shirley and said, "Would you like a job?" It was six days before her fourteenth birthday, but she agreed. She started the next week in the hospital laundry, moving into a room on the third floor of the hospital facing the Old Grove.

Coming from a busy family of ten, Shirley loved the independence of having her own room, meals in the hospital kitchen, and a salary of $50 per month. Every payday, she would go to the hospital booth to buy a Denver Sandwich chocolate bar, a bottle of Orange Crush, a tube of toothpaste, and the latest edition of Modern Screen magazine. She felt like she was living large.

Along with many of the other laundry girls, Shirley had to attend night school until she was sixteen. Two evenings a week, they went to the high school to learn typing. It was a drag to spend their evenings in class, so they got out of it whenever they could—Luxton Thuell, the laundry boss, be-

Shirley (standing second from the left) and the laundry girls.

came accustomed to seeing the school truancy officer coming across the hospital lawn to the laundry. He would call out, "Girls! Have you been missing school again?" They never got more than a stern talking-to.

At the time, the dance halls were the places to be. On Tuesday and Saturday, Barclay Square downtown would be hopping, and on Thursday night the crowds flocked to the Blue Room on Wellington Street. However, the highlight of the week was the Crystal Palace Ballroom in Mitchell on Friday night, when the Ranch Boys and CKNX set toes tapping all evening long. The afternoon before, Shirley and her girlfriends would stop in at the Sally Shop downtown to buy a new skirt and blouse for the occasion. Then, they'd walk down in their new duds to the Huron Street bridge to hitch a ride to Mitchell. The dance-floor was always packed. When the night ended, they never had to worry about getting a ride home because it seemed that half of Stratford was at the dance.

Shirley married at sixteen and had one son. The marriage lasted eight months. Several years later, she met Roy Pautler, who had just returned from military service in Korea in 1952. They married and raised five children together. That didn't put a stop to her dancing days, though—in fact, Shirley can still be found line dancing with the Stratford Lakeside Active Adults.

A Wartime Childhood
Arthur Wilson

Arthur sat at his dining room table eating break-fast. Beside his plate of toast and jam sat his baseball glove with the softball clenched inside. It was a warm spring day, and he was anxious to practise his pitching. In the other room, the radio was playing while his mother tidied the kitchen. Suddenly the program was interrupted by the an-nouncer's voice.

"Prime Minister Churchill announced at 2:31 this morning that the war is over, and Germany has unconditionally surrendered."

There was a moment of silence in the house, as Arthur looked at his mother in disbelief. Then, their faces broke into wide smiles. Arthur whooped, and in his exuberance, tossed the softball into the air. It went sailing through the picture window, smashing a pane as it fell, but neither he nor his mother paid any attention.

Arthur Wilson was only a boy during the Second World War, at that particular age when children are sponges, soaking up everything that they see and hear. Like most of his chums at the time, he had a voracious interest in anything war-related, from the radio shows which dramatized the missions of the Lancaster pilots to the tales of returning veterans in his own hometown.

Arthur's family was very involved in their town of Perth, Ontario, where his father was a High Court judge and his mother was president of the local International Order of the

Daughters of the Empire chapter. At the outset of the war, going-away parties for the soldiers were often hosted in his backyard, which would be bedecked with Union Jack flags and bunting. He recalls looking with admiration at the Air Force men, in their hats and wings, the army men with their impressive weapons glinting in their holsters, and the navy men in their dark blue bell-bottoms. Those parties were happy affairs, filled with plenty of beer, singing, and good wishes. It wasn't until later that the tragic reality set in— one third of the men they bid farewell to would never return.

Arthur and his buddies were only too glad to pitch in whenever they could, and as Arthur says, "there was always a campaign." On Saturday mornings, they were given the task of collecting any scrap metal they could find. They combed the city for old fences, unused implements, and anything else gathering dust in the back of their garages. By the end of the day, there was a mountain of metal in front of the armoury. This was all melted down to make artillery for the front lines.

Later in the war, there was another campaign which sought to collect milkweed to be used to make parachutes. Arthur got a big burlap sack and tied it into a bag, then spent the day at the edge of town collecting milkweed pods. He and his friends amassed a significant collection which was sent by train to Hamilton. Whether those pods ever ended up in parachutes drifting above Europe, he never did find out.

Ordinary residents helped in other ways as well. Nearly everyone kept a Victory Garden stocked with every kind of vegetable, which they would preserve for the winter in their fruit cellars. Booklets of food stamps controlled the sale of eggs, meat, and milk. When her friends came to visit, Arthur's mother would take her stamps out of the top drawer of the buffet and deal back and forth for the ingredients she needed. Gas, too, was rationed. At the pump, the gas for farmers was tinted a reddish colour, while the gas for everyone else who needed it for their employment (primarily businessmen, doctors, and lawyers) was yellow.

Townspeople kept abreast of the news through the radio. Arthur remembers sitting alongside his parents listening to a speech by Adolf Hitler broadcast from Berlin. "He didn't so much speak as scream," Arthur recalls. It was terrifying. He also remembers listening to the famous words of British Prime Minister Winston Churchill after the Battle of Britain, delivered in slow, measured tones: "Never in the field of human conflict has so much been owed by so many to so few." Many of the entertainment programs also had a war theme. Arthur would hurry to the radio when he heard the familiar drone of engines, signalling the beginning of "L for Lanky," a program which told stories of Lancaster bombing raids. Those tales would give inspiration to the backyard war games he and his friends loved to play.

The town railroad tracks were always a busy place, and the boys liked to loiter out near them to watch the cargo travelling in both directions. The next town down the tracks manufactured tanks which would pass by on flat cars bound for Halifax. They were covered by a tarp, but the barrel stuck out so the boys could identify them. In the other direction, passenger cars carried German prisoners of war on their way to camps somewhere in Ontario. The boys would yell curses at them as they passed.

The town was "great for parades" during the war, but by far the most joyful of them all happened spontaneously on Victory in Europe (VE) Day. When they heard of the war's end, the band members ran to the band shell and strapped on their instruments, leading the march down the street. Previously, Arthur had never seen rolls of toilet paper—it always came in individual sheets in a box. On VE Day, it suddenly materialized, festooning the street. One roll landed in the horn on the big brass tuba, bobbing jauntily up and down the street.

The war brought the veterans home, many returning with

duffel bags full of "loot" that they had picked up on the battlefield. Arthur and his friends would stare wide-eyed at the collections of Nazi flags, helmets, rifles, and guns that the veterans brought back from the front. One day, Arthur's friend called him over to his house. His father had somehow managed to smuggle home four duffel bags full of Luger pistols, one of the finest weapons of the war, and they were testing them out in their backyard. "The neighbours must have thought the war had started again," Arthur laughs.

The police stopped by to investigate the noise, but when realized the situation, they went on their way with only a light-hearted caution. For adults, the pistol didn't have much of a kickback, but for twelve-year-old Arthur, it was strong enough to rattle his teeth. He spent the afternoon doing target practice with a real Nazi pistol, the war games he played with his friends becoming more real with every shot. Years later, he would join the military himself, taking his place among the veterans whom he had so ardently admired as a child.

"All the good the past has had"
Violet Mohr

In the warm yellow lamplight, Violet and her mother worked quietly, each bent over their own task. The rest of the family was tucked into their beds in their farmhouse near Amulree, a small hamlet north of Shakespeare. The only sound was the fire crackling in the woodstove. Her mother's silver needle bobbed in and out between the dark wool of the socks she was darning. At the kitchen table, Violet was bent over a large sheet of paper, concentrating carefully as she dipped the paintbrush and swirled it across the page. The light caught the shimmer of gold paint on her canvas. Though her days were busy with farm work, at night she found time for her artwork.

Every morning when she was growing up, Violet Mohr's father would stand at the bottom of the stairs at six a.m. and holler, "All Aboard!" Soon after, his four children would scramble down and follow him out to the barn, where they each helped with the morning chores. Violet remembers milking the cows, turning the cream separator, and feeding the hens in the hen stable each morning, before setting off on the hour-long walk to school. Though she grew up in the "dirty thirties," Violet has only good memories of her childhood.

Their farm in Amulree was the centre of her world, and everything she needed was close by. There were two small stores within walking distance, which neighbours jokingly nicknamed "Simpson's" and "Eaton's" after the rival department stores found in the city. As kids, she and her siblings played every outdoor game they could come up with. One of their favourite things to do was walk on stilts that their father fashioned for them out of boards.

Violet (right) skating on the pond.

Violet clearly remembers begging to be allowed to go to school when she was five. In those days, new students began in the spring after Easter break. She didn't turn six until July, but she couldn't wait another year to join her siblings in the classroom. At first, her mother would not relent, believing that Violet was too small for the daily walk. However, her father stepped in, saying, "If she wants to go this badly, you'd better let her."

Each school day began with recitation of the Lord's Prayer and the reading of a Bible verse. There were 60 students in Violet's one-room schoolhouse when she began, so they had to sit two to a desk. Violet enjoyed every subject; even if she hadn't been assigned homework, she would often stay up after the day's work was done to study her lessons. She grew to know her readers inside-out and still remembers many of the verses she had to recite.

Early every Saturday morning, the family would load

S.S. No.5 Ratzburg in 1933.
Violet is in the first row, fourth from the left.

their wagon with produce and drive into Stratford to the market. After they had sold their goods, Violet had a chance to visit Kenner's Book Store on Ontario Street. There she purchased one of her most prized possessions: silver and gold paint. Nobody else in her class had them, and they added an extra shine to her artwork. Upon viewing some of her paintings, the school inspector even suggested that she continue her studies to become an artist.

At the end of the year, grade eight students from the country schools travelled to Milverton to write their entrance exams into high school. Of the 100 students who tried their exams, only ten passed with honours—and Violet was among them. However, there was no way for her to get to high school in town, so her formal education ended there. Still, her learning continued on the farm. "There wasn't much we didn't know how to do," she says. They managed without Hydro until 1946. She remembers the first tractor which her father and uncle purchased together—it was orange, and its metal wheels were covered with cleats. It couldn't even drive on the road, but it certainly helped with the threshing. With the tractor, they could do their own threshing instead of having to pile the sheaves of wheat in the barn and wait for the custom threshing machine to come around.

The community was tight-knit, and they always gathered for wedding showers and other celebrations. A group of local boys was usually on hand to provide the music, and Violet ended up marrying the banjo player. After her marriage, she did not stray far from Amulree; in fact, she moved to the farm just across the road. Years later, she and her husband Hilbert passed the farm on to their son and moved to a smaller house next door in Amulree.

From her kitchen window, she can still see the barn built by her great-grandfather on her family homestead. Now ninety years old, she often thinks fondly of her childhood days, bringing to mind one of her favourite lines of poetry by John Greenleaf Whittier:

> All the good the past has had
> Remains to make your own time glad.

Love and Bugs in the Bush
Shirley McPhee

It was four in the morning, but the girls in the laboratory of the Algoma Steel Plant were hard at work, balancing scales and measuring steel samples from the factory. They were busy pre-testing the steel and measuring it against other samples to ensure the ingredients were in their proper proportion. It was a man's job, but the war had taken most men away, leaving girls like Shirley to fill their roles. Like many of the workers there, she was only a teenager, having taken the job straight out of high school. For such young women, they carried a great deal of responsibilty on their shoulders; the steel was used to make rails for train tracks which were shipped across the world, and one single mistake could cost thousands of dollars. Nevertheless, the girls took on the challenge with youthful enthusiasm and proved themselves to be more than equal to the task.

Shirley McPhee spent her childhood years in North Bay, passing much of her time in the schoolyard playing with the neighbourhood children. Their games were simple and inventive— 'Run, Fish, Run' and 'Stoplight' were the favourites. Shirley and her cousins loved to put on plays in their backyard, using the clothesline as a stage curtain and charging ten cent's admission. For one production of *Rapunzel,* she cut her mother's yellow nightgown into strips and fashioned them into a wig which served as the essential long locks. Many hours of her childhood were spent at the candy store, poring over the options to determine the best way to spend her weekly allowance of 25 cents. On Saturdays, she would accompany her friends to confession and then head across the street to buy a dime's worth of peanuts and a ticket to the afternoon show. *Alice in Wonderland* was the first movie she ever saw.

Shirley (top right) with some close friends.

In high school, Shirley excelled in chemistry and aspired to be a lab technician after graduation. When the opportunity arose to work in the research lab of Algoma Steel, she was eager to begin. Together with many other girls, she rode the bus in for her shift every day, dressed like a man and never balking at the dirtiness of the job. She enjoyed the camaraderie and the challenge of the work, but when the war ended, she had to give up the position to returning veterans. Like all of the women, she accepted this reality—although it was a great disappointment to go from $100 a month at Algoma to 25 cents an hour at her next job.

Shirley soon found work at another laboratory where the subject of study was insects rather than steel. Now living in

Sault Ste. Marie, she joined a pioneering group of scientists in the brand new entomology labs which were established for insect research in northern Ontario. Led by Dr. Carl Atwood (the author Margaret Atwood's father), the lab was particularly concerned with monitoring the spruce budworm and forest tent caterpillar populations. It was staffed by lab technicians, many of whom were veterans who had returned to university after their overseas service. One of these technicians later became Shirley's husband. They worked alongside each other for a year without ever going on a date. It seemed that everyone else in the laboratory noticed their particular chemistry before they did. "We were sizing each other up, and we didn't even know it," Shirley recalls.

Her husband worked out in the bush, collecting insect samples which would be sent back to the lab for Shirley and the other lab assistants to catalogue and preserve. The insects would first have to be killed in an acid bath. Next, Shirley would stretch their wings and pin them to a board for display. Each one was individually labelled with its Latin name and host tree, which Shirley soon memorized. The boards were arranged by category in flat glass boxes and kept for reference, forming the beginnings of a complete record on insect populations in northern Ontario.

One day after work, Shirley asked the handsome lab technician for a ride to pick up a suitcase that she needed for an upcoming trip. Just before dropping her off, the technician leaned over and asked, "Do you like to live in the bush?" Though she was a city girl, she responded that she loved it. As it turned out, that was her wedding proposal. Her husband-to-be was sent north for the summer, conducting research in the bush. She visited him at his cabin only once, chaperoned by an elderly couple. It was through letters that they became close, learning about each other and beginning to share plans for the future. When they met again the following November, he presented her with a diamond ring.

They were married on Valentine's Day. Their courtship may have been an unusual one, but their marriage was happy and long, lasting for over sixty years.

Although she stopped working in the lab after her marriage, Shirley remained in close contact with the northern forests, often accompanying her husband on his trips into the bush. She became accustomed to keeping house in a government cottage outfitted with little more than an iron cot and an icebox. Sometimes, the accomodations were even more rustic. Shirley remembers waking up one night to hear rustling outside their tent. "Go back to sleep," her husband reassured her. "It's just the moose crossing on their trail."

Eventually, her husband's insect research took him from the quiet peace of the forest to the noise and activity of Toronto. They raised their growing family in the city, but brought the kids each year to their cabin in the woods, which was a summer playground for the family. Though many years have passed since those days, she has never lost her fondness for the North. Many of the first years of her married life were spent in the bush, and just as she had promised, she did love it.

Shirley and her husband at their cabin.

The Truth About California
Jane White

The four young women stepped off the train, exhausted but eager to see their new home. Their journey had taken them from small-town Stratford across the United States to San Francisco. It was the first time any of them had been on an airplane, and despite the many stop-overs, the experience of flying through the mountains had been thrilling. They crossed the Golden Gate Bridge and travelled by train to the city of Stockton. They were on their way to San Joaquin County Hospital, where they had accepted positions as nurses.

The women were under strict instructions that upon their arrival in Stockton, they should wait to be picked up by hospital officials. Under no conditions were they permitted to leave the station. Peering from the station's windows at the city outside, they soon realized why—far from the land of milk and honey that they had imagined, they found themselves in the middle of skid row.

Jane White enrolled in Stratford General Hospital Nursing School in 1951 when she was eighteen. She moved from her family farm north of London into the nurses' residence next door to the hospital. She and the twenty other young ladies in her class called the residence home for the next three years of their nursing studies.

Their schooling began with three months of lectures, before beginning hands-on work in the hospital itself. At first, the timid nurses found interacting with patients rather nerve-wracking, but it soon became natural. Jane and her peers worked six days a week, following a rigorous schedule. Mornings from seven until eleven were spent caring for patients in the hospital. Next, students would have lectures from eleven until three p.m. They would return to the hospital to finish the day, working from three until seven. During this first year, students were paid $36 a month, from which $30 was deducted for room and board. After a long day on their feet, they were left with little energy or money for anything besides supper at the residence cafeteria and homework.

During their second year of training, the nurses were delighted at the legislation of a mandatory eight hour workday, which shortened their shift to 7 am to 3 p.m. They also enjoyed a pay raise of $1 a month, as well as one extra day off every other week. To complete their training, nursing students spent time working at Sick Kids Hospital in Toronto to learn paediatrics, as well as London's Ontario Hospital to learn about the treatment of mental illness.

There wasn't much opportunity for mischief in the nurses' residence. The nursing superintendant and the nursing supervisor lived in rooms near the front door so they could keep a close eye on everyone's comings and goings. Both women were spinsters who were strict and set in their ways. They enforced a nightly curfew—the doors would lock nightly at 11 p.m. Each evening, one girl was assigned to sit by the door, admitting suitors and fetching their girlfriends from their rooms in the residence. The front lobby served as a sitting room where girls could visit with their boyfriends, but the boys were not permitted beyond the door to the dormitories.

Nevertheless, there was fun to be had when time permitted. Some girls would amuse themselves by trying on hats at Shapiro's Dress Shop downtown, while others would visit the candy shop or see a show at one of the movie theatres.

The Stratford Caffe on Ontario Street was a popular gathering spot where the nursing students would often mingle with apprentices from the CNR shops. The nursing school frequently held dances, and they would call over to the CNR shops to invite some of the apprentices to be partners. Jane met her future husband, then a CNR apprentice, one summer evening at the Stratford Caffe.

After graduation, Jane stayed on at Stratford General Hospital as a full time nurse. After a few months, she spotted a job posting from a hospital in California in the College of Nurses' newsletter. At the thought of California, Jane envisioned endless sunshine, mountains of gold, and a world of adventure compared to small-town Ontario. With these hopes in mind, Jane and three friends applied for the positions. In January 1955, they found themselves working for San Joaquin County Hospital.

They quickly realized that it was vastly different from what they had expected. The county hospital serviced only those who were unable to afford the fees for a private hospital, so most of their patients came from great poverty. The hospital itself was in the middle of the hot, dry countryside, next to the county jail.

The majority of inhabitants of San Joaquin County were grape-pickers, who were migrant workers living in desperate conditions. Their homes were hardly more substantial than a cardboard box, and most had only one possession to their name—their long grape-cutting knife. The nurses treated diseases and parasites that they had never encountered at home in Ontario.

Far from the land of plenty that Jane and her friends had envisioned, California turned out to be a much bleaker world. Three months later, Jane was on a plane back to Canada, one adventure under her belt, ready to begin a long career of nursing in southwestern Ontario.

From Alexandria to Algiers
Howard Bexton

Howard squinted in the morning sun as he emerged from his tent and pushed back the mosquito netting. His back ached from sleeping on nothing but a rubber mat, and yesterday's sunburn pricked his cheeks. Already, it was 102 degrees Fahrenheit, and it promised to get warmer as the day progressed. He was tempted to have a sip of water, but he ignored the instinct, knowing that the single bottle he had needed to last all day. It was never enough to stave off the insidious thirst that the desert provoked, but the nearest water was 60 miles away so there was no alternative.

He grimaced when he thought about breakfast, already knowing it would consist of bully beef and hard crackers, just like supper the night before, and lunch before that. He was a ground crewsman for the 417 Squadron RCAF Spitfires, and they were stationed outside Benghazi, Libya—far from the comforts of his Stratford home. With each British advance up the coast of North Africa, they followed, always ready at a moment's notice to help the Spitfires with landing or take-off. As the others in the tent began to stir, Howard started to pack up, preparing to move camp again that day. With each move they got a little bit closer to victory in the campaign.

Howard Bexton's parents travelled by boat from England to Canada in 1909, settling in Stratford to raise their five children. Thirty-two years later, their son was headed in the other direction to serve in the Second World War. Howard joined the Air Force in 1939 at the age of eighteen. His plans of being a pilot were quashed by colour-blindness, so instead he learned to be an airframe mechanic at the Technical Training School in St. Thomas. The school had been established to prepare the masses of new recruits required for the war effort, and a total of fifty thousand men trained there over the course of the war. Here, Howard was assigned his military number, R90164.

Howard is in the middle row, fourth from the left.

As soon as Howard completed his training, he volunteered for overseas duty. On December 13, 1941, his boat left the Halifax harbour bound for Liverpool. The crossing was very rough, and on the thirteen-day trip, Howard lost thirteen pounds. The waters of the Atlantic were fraught with the danger of U-boats lurking beneath the surface, so it was necessary to keep life belts on at all times. They were relieved to see the cliffs of England in the distance the day after Christmas.

They spent two months in England, unsure where they would be sent next. When they were issued desert clothes, the rumour circulated that Australia might be their destination. They soon found otherwise. The next boat they boarded took them around the Cape and docked in South Africa. Another boat carried them up to Cairo. They were forced to take this circuitous route because the Mediterranean was under German control at that time.

They joined the British Eighth Army under General Montgomery in Alexandria, Egypt, uniting with three squadrons of Spitfires—36 aircrafts in total. Spitfires were fast, high-altitude fighter planes equipped with 20 mm cannons on the wings as well as four machine guns. Their task was generally to fly above bombers and protect them from enemy planes. Whenever they got a notice that the enemy was coming, the ground crew would spring into action preparing them for take-off. Finding ground hard enough to serve as a runway was not always easy in the desert sand, but they made do, sometimes even sitting on the tailplate as the aircraft gained speed to weigh it down. Howard and his crewmates accompanied the British advance from Alexandria all the way to Algiers.

The hostile environment seemed to be working against them on their trek. They had to contend with sandstorms that could last for several days, insects carrying unfamiliar diseases, and the stifling, inescapable heat. At night, the men would zip themselves into their tents never knowing how long they would be able to sleep until the sirens began. They dug trenches outside their tents where they would hunker down, buckle on their helmets, and wait. The bombs always fell at night, except for one occassion outside Benghazi. They were travelling through the desert when—without warning—a bomb exploded near them, leaving a hole the size of a house where there had once been flat sand. It had been dropped by a German plane in order to lighten its load and facilitate its escape from an Allied plane which was pursuing it. The group suffered remarkably little damage from the explosion, but the fluke occurrence left a permanent mark on one of Howard's crewmates. His hair turned from brown to pure white after the incident.

Howard (left) on his way to his squadron's reunion.

The fighting was especially fierce outside of Tripoli, a large harbour city. Howard and the aircraft crew were staying in a former German aerodrome outside of the city. Every night, the German planes would fly over and bomb the area. Sleep was impossible, with the sirens blaring, the planes flying overhead, and the "ack-ack" (anti-aircraft) guns firing back their response while the shrapnel crashed down on the corrugated steel roof. The sky was lit up with flares and searchlights, and danger was omnipresent. Finally, the Axis forces in North Africa were defeated. Howard recalls watching a long line of German prisoners of war filing past him, heading south while Howard was heading north. Their job in North Africa was done.

Next, Howard returned to Liverpool, just in time for the D-Day invasion. He spent the weeks before June 6, 1944 working nearly non-stop to prepare bombers for their missions. The planes would take off from the aerodrome in the middle of England around mid-afternoon and head south where the fighter planes would join them to offer protection as they fulfilled their missions over France or Holland.

The anticipation and hope surrounding the invasion was palpable, fuelling them through their round-the-clock work. When the day finally arrived, all the telephones at the air base were taken to the front guard station and chained up, a precaution against any information being leaked. D-Day set in motion the gears of victory, and at last Howard was sent home. He arrived in December 1944, grateful to be back on the familiar streets of Stratford after experiencing another world overseas.

The Snake Surprise
Bernice Richards

It was shortly after eight in the morning when the young teacher hurried up the path to the one-room schoolhouse. She liked to arrive well before the students to write the morning lessons on the chalkboard and prepare for the day of juggling eight different grades at once. She had just reached the door when she stopped short.

There, curled around the door handle, was a long snake.

The young woman stiffened, but quickly stifled her gasp. She was petrified of snakes, but she also suspected that there were some young eyes peeking out from behind the woodpile. Immediately, she realized that the snake's presence on the doorknob was the product of some early-morning mischief by the grade seven and eight boys. She remembered the familiar advice from teachers' college: as long as you're strict with the children the first week, you'll have no trouble for the rest of the year. Taking a deep breath, she picked up a stick from beside the path. With the calmest demeanour she could muster, she removed the snake and continued into the classroom without batting an eye.

For the rest of the year, the grade seven and eight boys gave her no more trouble.

Bernice Richards was raised outside of Atwood and moved to Stratford in 1955 to attend teachers' college. Interspersed with her studies, she completed placements in Kitchener, Guelph, and several country schools. She soon learned that her calling was in the country.

After graduation, she secured a position in a one-room school outside of Ethel, where she taught 24 pupils across eight grades. Managing such a wide range of learning levels was a skill that she picked up quickly. Her lesson plans always involved a lot of multi-tasking. While the older kids were writing out their spelling words, she would lead the middle grades in spelling dictation, and supervise the littlest pupils in a colouring activity. For some subjects such as social studies, two grades learned together, making her job slightly easier.

Around exam time, Bernice would spend hours labouring over the hectograph, a flat rectangular device with a jelly pad inside, which preceded today's photocopier. First, she had to write out the exam questions with a purple pencil, then press that sheet onto the dampened jelly pad for several minutes. When the paper was removed, it left an impression—rather like a large stamp. It was a very long process just to ensure that all students had their own exam paper.

By the time the weekend rolled around, Bernice was ready for a break. On any given Saturday night, one of the small towns in the area would be holding a dance, and chances were good that Bernice and her husband would be in attendance. Their relationship had begun on the dancefloor, shortly after Bernice graduated from high school. One December evening, Bernice and her friend were torn between attending the dance in Mitchell and the dance in Ethel. For her part, Bernice was hoping to go to Mitchell. She had just broken up with her boyfriend, and she was hoping to see him there, secretly angling for a reconciliation. However, her friend was the stronger-willed of the two, so they found themselves on the road to Ethel.

They'd been there for a little while when a rowdy group

of young men came in, on their way home from the hockey game. One of them, named Jerry, asked her to dance. As they were circling the dance floor, Bernice began to notice something peculiar. All the older ladies in the room were glaring in their direction. After a few moments, they realized it was because Jerry's boots were leaving black streaks across the dance floor. Embarrassed, he hurried home to change his footwear, returning in time to accompany Bernice home that night. Nearly 55 years later, they can still be found on the dance floor in small towns across the county.

After their marriage the Richards moved into Stratford, but Bernice continued to teach out in the country schools of Gadshill and Hampstead. That was where she got her start, and the one-room schoolhouses were always where her teaching passion resided.

War Work and Worry

Frances Lawson

*It was nearly seven o'clock, and Kroehler Fur-
niture Factory was buzzing with the usual morning activity. By all accounts, it was an ordinary
day—however, in some ways, it was very out-of-
the-ordinary indeed. Instead of chesterfields and
armchairs, the factory was churning out spars for
the Mosquito bomber plane. And instead of the
usual men in the workshops and warehouses, the
factory was staffed nearly entirely by women. It
was the year 1942, and Stratford was marshalling
all of its resources to further the war effort overseas.*

*Frances joined the line of women preparing
to start their workday. They were dressed iden-
tically in navy blue slacks, light blue shirts, and
vests that tied around the back. Their long hair
was pulled back into kerchiefs, and most carried a
lunch pail. As they waited, they chatted amiably.
Like Frances, many had boyfriends or husbands
overseas, and they all shared in the worry and
loneliness of being the one left at home.*

*At the front of the line, they showed their pass
card to the Air Force guard and proceeded to their
work stations. All day long, they carried out their
work diligently, hoping that somehow their con-
tribution would help to bring the war to an end.*

Frances Lawson was born in Stratford in 1925, the daughter of a milkman. Of her childhood, she recalls summer nights

spent by the Avon River, watching the concerts in the band shell or peeking in the windows of the Casino Dance Hall to watch the couples swaying back and forth to the music. When she was old enough herself, she would attend the jitney dances there. Young men with long lines of five-cent tickets would stroll up the row of benches where the ladies sat, eyeing up their prospective partners. For each dance, they would have to pay one five-cent ticket to be admitted onto the dance floor. After the song ended, couples would be herded off the floor and had to give another ticket for the next dance. Every Tuesday, Thursday, and Saturday night in the summer, the river path would be alive with couples strolling arm in arm while the music and laughter from the dance hall filtered across the water.

Frances was sixteen when Stratford welcomed Dutch soldiers taking refuge from occupied Europe. They spent over a year living in the barracks of a converted furniture factory, completing their training in the safety of small-town Ontario until they were prepared to fight overseas. Many of the officers brought their families along and rented homes in the area, employing local girls as housekeepers and babysitters. Frances worked for a Dutch officer and his wife one summer. They rented a cottage in Grand Bend, and she lived there as their housemaid. Every morning, the officer would drive from Grand Bend to Stratford and return at night, leaving his military obligations behind to spend the evening on the shores of Lake Huron.

After grade eleven, Frances left school to work at the Bentro Knitting Company. The war had greatly increased the demand for knitted gloves for soldiers, so the company rented out the top storey of a car showroom across the street to expand their operations. She was still in training there when she heard about the night classes that Kroehler's and Imperial Rattan furniture factories were holding. Both factories were making spars, the wooden framework for the wing

44

in the Mosquito airplane. Overrun with war contracts, they were desperately in need of skilled workers, so they sponsored free classes in carpentry for local women. Since the pay for a knitter-in-training was only $5 a week, Frances was happy for a new opportunity. She went with her sister and a friend to enroll in carpentry classes, and before long, they were students at Beal Technical School in London. They spent ten weeks there, heading to class after the high school students were gone and spending the evening working with the chisel and plane, learning how to measure with exactitude, and practising carpentry techniques.

When they finished, Frances and her sister were both hired at Kroehler's, working for 50 cents an hour which was then a generous wage. Frances' job was scarfing—using a plane to taper the wood down to an end. This filled her time from seven in the morning until six at night, six days a week. On Saturdays, they were finished an hour earlier. That was the only night they could do their shopping, so the stores downtown stayed open late, often until 11 p.m.

At the end of a long day, Frances would hurry home to the mailbox, hoping for a letter from her boyfriend who was serving in the Navy. He spent the war travelling between Londonderry, Ireland, and St. John's, Newfoundland, protecting the merchant ships on their perilous Atlantic crossings. The time in between letters was often long.

In addition to making spars, Kroehler's also had a contract to repair Tiger Moths, the flimsy training planes used at air force bases such as Port Albert and Ipperwash. Frances also worked in the area where the planes would come to be repaired. They were small and simple machines which bore a poignant resemblance to the wooden model airplanes that young boys grew up playing with.

When the damaged planes were brought into the factory, they would sometimes be caked with mud and grass from the crash. They had to be cleaned and patched. The

Frances (far right) and her co-workers attending a dance class. Kroehlers rented the YMCA for its staff members one night a week.

sewing rooms which had formerly made furniture coverings were re-purposed to sew linen covers that Frances and the other workers would pull over the wings, affixing them as tightly as possible. After that, the plane would be sent to the paint booth, which would stiffen the linen. Ready for flight again, they would then be returned to the bases by train. When Frances watched the planes flying overhead, she always marvelled that something that seemed hardly stronger than a matchstick could hold together in the air.

By 1944, spar production at Kroehler's was winding down, so Frances moved to Toronto to work in a factory which made paper cups for military canteens. She lived with her grandmother and worked alongside her aunt in the factory. Midway through the day on May 7, 1945, the word came that the war was over. Any thought of work was abandoned, and the streets filled quickly as nearly everyone in the city took the afternoon off. Along with thousands of others, Frances made her way downtown.

Frances and her boyfriend.

The scene was unforgettable. Union Jacks dangled from every window, paper confetti gathered in the gutters like fresh snow, and placards proclaimed, "GERMANY SURRENDERS" in triumphant letters. Every few blocks, the streetcar would jolt to a stop because in the midst of the celebrations, the wire connecting the car to electricity was pulled out. Each time, the driver would have to walk back and re-connect it, but even he didn't grumble. There was a spirit of pure joy in the air.

The end of the war also brought Frances' boyfriend home at last. He had been on leave in London when peace was announced, experiencing the happy chaos of VE Day in Trafalgar Square. On his return to Canada, a U-boat surfaced and surrendered to his ship—the first U-boat of the war to surrender after VE day.

During his one month leave, he and Frances got married. He had to return to be 'mustered out,' then at last, the two moved back to Stratford to set up their home. Over the course of the war, the letters sent between them had accumulated into stacks and bags of white envelopes. In their new house in Stratford, they burned the letters in the kitchen stove, glad to put the sorrow of the war behind them as they embarked on their new life together.

The New Year's Eve Puppy
Vesta Wahl

Vesta turned a corner in the barn and stopped short. Tucked behind the hay mow, the family dog was reclined, surrounded by five tiny puppies. Their fur was short and spiky, and they made a mewling sound as they burrowed clumsily towards their mother. Vesta could tell they were only a few days old because their eyes were still closed.

She backed silently out of the room, careful not to draw any attention to the puppies. She knew that her father, ever the pragmatic farmer, would not allow those puppies to remain there if he knew their whereabouts. However, even he had a soft spot; once their eyes were opened, he couldn't kill them. Sharing a conspiratorial look with the mother dog as she left, she turned and quietly exited the barn.

Vesta Wahl was born on a farm in Downie township which was located on a corner lot. In 1921, all the babies born on those four corners were afflicted with infant paralysis, now known as polio. It hit Vesta's younger brother especially hard, and he never learned to walk or talk as a result. He needed all of his mother's care, so one-year-old Vesta was sent to live on her grandparents' nearby farm. She didn't move home until she was six, to attend the school which was located directly on the family farm.

The big event in the school year was the Fall Fair. Students from all the schools in Downie would converge at the township hall in St. Paul's for the festivities. They would bring vegetables which had been painstakingly picked and cleaned—rows of uniform carrots or plates of round potatoes to be judged. If their vegetables didn't win them a ribbon, they could try their luck in foot races and other competitions. All the schools, from S.S.#3 through S.S.#10, would march in a parade, which was also judged. S.S.#6, which Vesta attended, always won first prize.

Though it was uncommon at the time, Vesta's mother insisted that she go on to high school. She took her entrance exams along with nine others in her class. All nine passed—although the stress was so much for one boy that he fainted and didn't have to try his exams. After high school in Stratford, Vesta returned to her parents' farm. She got a job across the river at the creamery, wrapping butter and caring for the owner's children. Her father placed stepping stones in the river so she could walk across without wetting her feet.

Every winter, the owner of the creamery made an ice rink in his field, which was a popular gathering spot for the neighbours. They would tie their horses in Vesta's father's barn and come across the river to lace on their skates for an evening on the ice. It was here that Vesta met her husband-to-be. She recognized him from the baseball games she'd attended in the summer, when his team from North Easthope township played against the Downie township team. They married in 1940, a time when anti-German sentiment was strong in the area. Since her husband was of German descent, Vesta's family no longer wanted anything to do with her after that.

The newlyweds' first home was a primitive farmhouse with no electricity in Logan township. They borrowed $50 to buy 15 pigs, fattened them with grain from the granary, and then sold them at market. After a few well-managed interactions like this, they were able to outfit their house with Hydro—the first one on their block to get it! Their

Vesta and her husband on their wedding day.

favourite pastime was playing cards. On Saturday evenings, they would light up the big gas lamp above the kitchen table and spend the evening playing euchre and rummy with the neighbours. Their life on the farm was cut short by a fluke accident. During a logging bee in the bush, Vesta's husband reached out to grab a falling log at the same time that his neighbour reached out with the axe, cutting off part of his hand.

After this, Vesta's husband was no longer able to do the farm work, so they moved to a smaller property and searched for a new livelihood. An idea took root one stormy New Year's Eve when the Wahl's became snow-bound at a neighbour's house for the night. The next morning, the neighbour gave them a tiny St. Bernard puppy. She did not stay tiny for long, and when she was fully grown the Wahls bred her. Her offspring were the first of hundreds of puppies to pass through their home, as they became registered breeders.

After many years of breeding St. Bernards, they moved

on to shelties and finally pugs. They soon became regulars on the dog show circuit as well as lifelong members of the Canadian Kennel Club. Meanwhile, Vesta's husband took a job at Riverside Silk Mills, repairing the looms in the weavery. He went wherever the looms went, so the family moved from Mitchell to Galt and then Dunnville. They raised two daughters, and Vesta worked in the office of an insurance company. When the office was moved, they asked if she would consider becoming a field underwriter, and thus she began her career selling insurance. Eventually, Vesta retired to Stratford with her husband and her last dog—a pug named Midgie.

A City for a Playground
Russ Brown

The young boys stood at the top of the hill, delight written all over their pink cheeks. It was late fall of 1953, and the inaugural season of the Stratford Festival had ended over a month ago. The crowds had dispersed, the wooden stage had been dismantled, and the great white tent collapsed and folded away for next year. All that was left was a series of passageways and holes carved into the ground which had formed the backstage walkways during the season. For most people, the excitement had passed, but for the children of Stratford, the fun was only just beginning.

The boys had not been very pleased to see the excavation beginning on the tent site that spring. They were dismayed to watch the best tobogganing run in the city being torn up. From their perspective, the eloquence of Shakespeare couldn't compete with the pure thrill of flying down the hill on their rickety wooden sleighs, sailing across the wide field, and finally skidding onto the frozen Avon River below. However, the sight before them was making them reconsider their earlier scepticism.

The rain had accumulated in the alleyways, pooling in the gullies and forming deep puddles at every corner. It was a muddy paradise that would make mothers cringe just thinking of the piles of laundry it would create. As the first few drops of rain fell, the boys looked at one another mis-

chievously. With wide grins, they hopped into the mucky hollow, slipping and sliding as they tore through the passageways, their giggles and shouts muffled by the rain.

Russ Brown grew up in the East End of Stratford, right in the heart of the manufacturing district. A stone's throw from his childhood home, Imperial and Kroehler's were churning out high quality solid-wood furniture while Preston-Noelting was shipping office furniture across the country. A few blocks away, Avon Knit made yarns, and Avalon Fabric produced upholstery for chesterfields. The Sealed Power plant was right in his backyard. When he was three years old, it caught on fire. He strained to watch the black smoke billowing out of the building and darkening the sky, but even a fire would not stop his mother from putting him down for his afternoon nap. He was miffed to have missed the excitement.

Like many others in the city, Russ's father worked at the Canadian National Railway shops. He was a crane operator, lifting the huge steam engines so that men could make repairs to the undersides. Russ's five uncles also worked in the shops as welders. The rail industry then was the lifeblood of the town, and the daily traffic of trains through the city core was simply a part of every day. Housewives living close to the track would learn to listen for the whistle of the steam engine and run out to grab their clothes off the line, to avoid them being sullied by the blast of soot released by the engine on its way through town. During the 1950s, Stratford's manufacturing heyday was beginning to wane, as steam engines were replaced by diesel engines. When the shops closed their doors in 1958, the town was devastated. Two hundred men lost their jobs, in addition to those who had already been phased out through the decade. The face of Stratford industry was left very changed.

However, these troubles were far from the minds of young boys. For them, the gritty industrial yards were nothing more than jungle gyms and obstacle courses. Russ and his gang of neighbourhood kids would climb in the piles of lumber out behind Kroehler's and play hide and seek in the out-of-commission steam cars at the rail yards. Another favourite pastime was exploring the storm sewers. Crawling into a culvert at the corner of Romeo and Douro Street, the boys would make their way underground all the way to the middle of the Juliet school grounds, climbing out before that pipe joined up with the main sewer that would have sent them straight into the Avon at Queen Street. It was dark and clammy down there, and there were all manner of slimy treasures for curious youngsters to discover. They crawled out of the sewers so smelly that nobody wanted to come near them.

As well as exploring underground, Russ and his friends also ventured in the other direction, climbing the four storey Imperial Furniture factory at night to gallivant on the rooftop. The view of the city—as well as the adrenaline rush—was magnificent. One night, there was a close call when in the midst of their play, one of the boys was heading straight for the edge of the roof. Russ reached out just in time to pull him back.

On summer nights, the ball diamond behind Kroehler's and Avalon Fabrics was busy with players and spectators. The factory had a men's and a ladies' team which competed against the other teams in "The Big Four:" Hamilton, Kitchener, and London. Russ's aunt played for the Kroehler Chicks, so the family often went down to watch the game. Russ would wait out behind the diamond, chasing foul balls. He brought them back in exhange for five cents each, which funded the occasional trip to the candy store. The baseball diamond has since been replaced by tennis courts.

As Russ and his friends grew up, their favourite haunts changed. From the sewers and rooftops, they moved on to Clarke's Pool Room—or the CPR as it was fondly known.

It was located on Wellington Street, making it a convenient spot for a few rounds of billiards between school and after-school jobs. He still spent many nights at the ball diamonds, but by then he had graduated from foul-ball retriever to player. After games, he and his teammates would head over to the Empire Hotel, the biggest dive in town, or the Mansion House to see if they could get served without ID.

After grade twelve, Russ was convinced that he had put his school days behind him. He took a job at Collins-Aikman, weaving upholstery fabric on a night shift. It didn't take long to realize that was not the life for him. He returned to grade thirteen and eventually spent many years in university. Though his sewer-roaming days are behind him, Russ is as active in Stratford as he was when he was a boy. He can still be found chasing balls on the baseball diamond.

Kroehler Furniture Factory in 1959.
Stratford Perth Archives Photograph.

Fort Erie Bound
Addie MacMillan

Addie watched from across the parking lot as her husband disappeared into the factory. A few hours ago, the family had left their farm near Gadshill before the sunrise was even brightening the horizon. The sky lightened as they drove to Fort Erie, pulling their newly-purchased house trailer behind them. By seven in the morning, they were parked in the lot of the factory, and her husband joined the line of men reporting for work that Monday morning. The factory was making Fairchild training planes for the war effort, and they needed all the help that they could get.

Addie turned back to the house trailer, where her toddler was sleeping. The two of them would have to spend the day here. With no running water or electricity, it was far more primitive than the farmhouse which she had left behind her. The sun was already beginning to warm the asphalt as Addie's son stirred and opened his eyes. It would be ten hours until her husband returned.

Born in 1915, Addie MacMillan grew up on a farm east of Gadshill, the youngest in a family of eleven children. Many of her childhood days were occupied with hoeing, an endless task since each rain brought a fresh crop of weeds sprouting between the rows of corn and potatoes. At night, the farmhouse was lively with music, as all three of Addie's brothers played the violin. They would often push the kitchen table off to the side, invite the neighbours, and hold a dance.

Addie is seated on her father's lap,
in front of her childhood home.

Addie left the farm at age 17, moving into Stratford to keep house for a well-to-do family with two children. She did everything from the childcare to the cooking, for a weekly wage of $3. Her sister worked in town as well, and on their day off they would return to the home farm for a visit. Not long after, their Sunday trips home also came to include a visit from a pair of brothers who lived on a nearby farm. After many double dates, both couples married.

In the 1930s, there was no money to fund a fancy wedding, so Addie and her husband-to-be were married in the parlour of the manse, with only the minister and his wife in attendance. The first years of their life together were spent working for a bachelor on his farm in North Easthope Township until they saved enough to purchase a farm of their own. There was no prosperity in farming at the time. The couple could hardly make any money from their cattle or milk sales, so it was a constant challenge to to stay ahead of the bills.

One afternoon, Addie's husband was outside fixing a motor when he looked up to see black smoke billowing out of the barn. Soon, flames were devouring the barn boards and turning the heavy beams to ash. Neighbours hurried over to help, but their buckets of water were powerless in halting the blaze. They could only stand in the smoky air with solemn faces, watching as the barn was consumed. Fortunately, the cows and horses had been out to pasture when it happened, so they lost only a few chickens. Though they eventually rebuilt the barn, the fire was devastating to the young couple.

In the early 1940s, Addie's husband decided to enlist to fight in the war. When he arrived at the recruiting office in London, he was presented with a different option. There was an aircraft factory in Fort Erie desperately in need of workers. They were manufacturing training planes, and there would be a position for him if he wanted it. His visit to the recruiting office took place on a Wednesday; he was expected to report for his first day of work the next Monday.

Instead of saying goodbye to her husband, Addie found herself saying goodbye to her farm. The next few days were a flurry of activity as they hurried to rent out their land and pack up the few belongings they could take with them. Housing was very short in Fort Erie, so they purchased a house trailer for their temporary accomodations. In only a few days, they had completely uprooted their lives and settled in an entirely new town. Back home in the rolling fields of North Easthope, the war had seemed very far away, but Fort Erie in wartime was "a bit spooky." Its proximity to the border meant that security was heightened. Addie grew to expect the sirens which would occasionally send them scrambling to extinguish their lights and cover their windows with dark curtains.

Addie began to work at the factory alongside her husband after her sister-in-law came to join them in Fort Erie. They would work opposite shifts so one of them was always home to care for the children. For a starting wage of 38 cents per hour, Addie worked 10 hour days as a welding fitter, filing the edges of metal pieces so they would fit snugly together. The welder she worked alongside was a woman as well, who had been trained for the job to fill the wartime trades shortage. Addie had fun working there because of all the new people she met; families from across the province found themselves in Fort Erie just as the MacMillans had, so everyone was a stranger. At the factory, they were allowed one weekend off each month, and Addie's husband would trade his beer rations for gas rations so the family could drive home to Perth County for a visit.

The job at the aircraft factory ended with the war and soon after the MacMillans left Fort Erie. Most people expected that they would return to the farm, but instead they moved to Toronto where Addie's husband got a job at Goodyear Tire. "People thought we were crazy, but we didn't miss the farm," Addie recalls. "We liked the adventures we had." In Toronto, the MacMillans welcomed another son to their family.

After Addie's husband retired, they moved to the shores of Lake Huron, where they rented out cottages and cabins near Sauble Beach. They enjoyed the winters the best, when the rowdy crowds of beachgoers went home and the snow fell thickly around their little house. Sometimes they were snowed in, but they didn't mind. After many years on those sandy beaches, the couple returned to Perth County, trading their cottage for a house trailer on Crystal Lake before moving into Stratford.

Learning Together
Isabel Plant

Isabel sat in front of the typewriter at the dining room table, frowning as she tried to decipher the scrawling handwriting on the paper in front of her. In the kitchen, her husband was pacing, pausing every now and then to write a few more lines on the paper on the table. His three-year-old son clung to his leg, while the other three children raced through the house in pursuit of their dog.

This was the scene of a typical Saturday evening as Isabel's husband entered his final year of theology studies at Emmanuel College. On Monday morning, he would make the commute back to Toronto for class, and it was imperative that the essay was finished.

"There!" Isabel finally exclaimed, pulling the last pages out of the typewriter. She and her husband bent over the table, proof-reading the paper before he tucked it away in his satchel among his textbooks. This week's deadline would be met.

Isabel Plant was born in Kingston, Ontario in the year 1926. Her father worked for the YMCA, and he had been sent to India during the First World War to organize recreational activities for the British troops stationed there. When it became clear that his stay would be an extended one, Isabel's mother travelled across the ocean to join him, their two-year-old daughter in tow. They had two more children in India before the war's end brought them back to Kingston. As a child, Isabel remembers watching the flickering slides of photographs from their travels time and time again, as they were frequently asked to talk about their trip to different organizations and community groups.

When she was six years old, the family moved to Kitchener. At the time, the well-known Kitchener businessman A.R. Kaufman was on the board of the YMCA, so he set the family up with a house. It faced Victoria Park, providing the children with many happy afternoons spent skating on the frozen lake. During the winter, lights were strung from a pole in the centre of the lake and music was played. Their time in that home was interrupted when Isabel's father's job was given to a local war hero, leaving her father unemployed. They purchased another house across the park, but it wasn't ready in time for the children to begin school in the fall.

In the interim, Mr. Kaufman let the family stay in his summer cottage in Bridgeport on the other side of the Grand River. It was quite a change from their pleasant city home—there was no electricity or running water. Every morning, her father would row the children across the Grand and drive them to school in the city. After two months, they were settled in their new home with a brand new appreciation for electric lights.

After graduating from high school, Isabel decided to become a nurse, completing her training at Hamilton General Hospital. Her brother, four years her senior, was attending the Ontario Veterinary College in Guelph at the time. His studies there had been put on hold by his war service in the Air Force, and he was in the process of finishing his degree. One evening, Isabel attended a dance at the college and was introduced to his friend Cliff. The two began dating and were married in 1949.

Isabel only practiced nursing for one year, because she quickly became immersed in a different job with its own challenges: raising four children born within six years. The young family moved into a new home next to Cliff's veterinary practice in St. Catherines. It was there that they started to become more active in church life, attending couples' club meetings each week. Then, they got the opportunity to attend a national conference which gathered couples' club members from many United Churches across Canada. Their growing involvement led Cliff to decide that he wanted to join the ministry.

This was a life-changing decision for the family. For the three years that Cliff would spend in school, the family would have to survive with no income, and Isabel would be left alone with the children all week. Afterwards, they would have to be prepared to go where the church sent them. After much deliberation and prayer, they agreed that it was the right thing to do. Cliff enrolled in the college, and so began three long years of lonely weeknights and harried weekends juggling homework and family. At the same time, Isabel was taking voice lessons, occasionally competing in the local Kiwanis Music Festival. It tested their mettle, but with Cliff's ordination, they emerged triumphantly.

Their first posting was in Lion's Head, a small town on the Bruce Peninsula which had seen many preachers come and go in recent years. After ordination, ministers were required to stay for two years in their assigned congregation, after which point they could apply to be moved. The Plants, however, loved the small-town atmosphere, and they remained there for six years. Their children became known as the "PKs," the Preacher's Kids. As minister's wife, Isabel assumed responsibility for leading the junior choir, while participating actively in all church activities.

Her involvement in the church grew over the years. When they returned to Kitchener, Cliff served as the minister of Christ the King Church for eight years. He also returned to school again for a two-year course on marriage counselling. He enjoyed it so much that Isabel decided to take the course as well. Later, they would run a marriage and family counselling business in Stratford.

Their church work took them next to North Bay, where Cliff was the personnel minister for the Manitou conference of churches. There, Isabel served as pastoral associate for St. Andrew's United Church of North Bay, visiting parishioners, organizing various groups, and helping with odd jobs in the church. She even conducted a funeral, although she was never ordained.

Upon their retirement, Isabel and her husband eventually moved to Stratford to be nearer to Isabel's older brother. Besides establishing their counselling business, they also began a new pursuit: learning and practicing Tai Chi, a Chinese system of meditative physical activity. Cliff died in 2010, but Isabel remains an active member of the Taoist Tai Chi Society of Stratford.

Born in a Blizzard
Walter Kollman

The door burst open, and the doctor entered, bringing a gust of cold wind with him. His coat was white with snow, and his eyes were buried beneath the thick wool hat he wore. To the young farmer pacing by the window, he could not have been a more welcome sight.

"Have you ever seen a storm like this?" the doctor exclaimed as he unravelled the snow-encrusted scarf from his face. "The car got stuck on the highway outside of Milverton. Thank goodness for your neighbour there with his cutter." He warmed his hands for a moment by the stove, then hurried up the stairs to the bedroom.

An hour later, a small cry drifted down the stairs, and the young man jumped to his feet. It was a baby boy who would follow in his father's footsteps to become a farmer.

The Kollman farm, where Walter moved soon after his birth, is found northeast of Stratford on Airport Road. Of course, there was no airport there when Walter was a child. Even cars were a limited form of transportation, since the winter snows made the roads impassable to all but the horse and cutter.

Walter grew up in the middle of the hustle and bustle of the farm. When he was six, he took the neighbour girl to show her the horses in the barn, and one of them unexpectedly bucked. His heavy, shod hoof caught Walter on the forehead, leaving him with a half-moon scar that is still

Walter as a baby.

visible today. By the age of nine, Walter was driving the family's new steel-wheeled 1937 Fordson tractor. He worked steadily alongside his father and his uncles all through his youth, thinking nothing of it. It was simply the way of life.

Every September, Walter cut across the fields to the tiny Brocksden School, where he and eleven other pupils attended classes. He remembers the yearly Christmas concert, when students would put on skits and musical performances which they practised under the guidance of the travelling music teacher. In North Easthope, the music teacher was Ida Kollman, Walter's aunt and a well-known figure in the community. She cultivated the musical talent of children in schoolhouses across the township on her weekly visits. Sixty years have passed since Walter's school days, but he still remembers his line from one of the plays they performed: "It gives me great pleasure to sit here and converse with you."

The students of Brocksden School.
Walter is on the far right in the middle row.

At the age of thirteen, Walter finished school and started to work on the farm full-time. When he was 16, he and his father formed a partnership and continued to farm together until Walter took over completely in 1968. During this time, many changes took place in the world of farming. After buying their first tractor, the Kollmans continued to use their horses occasionally. For some tasks, they were still the most convenient. During the fall threshing, the horses would walk from stook to stook while the men forked the wheat onto the wagon, which was much easier than repeatedly parking the tractor. They also used the team to do the scuffling in the spring. However, once they purchased a second tractor, the horses weren't needed much anymore. In those days, there was much more hand labour to be done on the farm. Even in the winter when the silos were full and the fields cleared, there was still lots of work feeding and watering the animals and mucking out their stalls.

The forties were a prosperous time to farm. Prices were

Threshing with horses and tractors.

always going up, compared to the volatile markets of today which fluctuate far more rapidly. In addition, farms were much smaller. When Walter was growing up, 12-20 cows were considered a good-sized herd. The Kollmans milked by hand and poured the fresh milk into the separator. The skim milk went to the pigs, and the cream was stored in cans in a cistern until it could be delivered to the creamery on Erie Street. They also kept chickens, candling and grading the eggs on the farm and delivering them each week to homes in Stratford.

Around the time that Walter took over the farm, the quota system came into effect. Quota seeks to cap production on such farm products as milk and eggs in order to keep prices steady; each farmer is alloted a quota for how much they may produce. At the outset of the program, farmers were granted free quota for whatever livestock they already had on their premises. Any operation with more than 500 chickens needed quota to operate, a threshold which has since been lowered. If the farmer didn't use his quota, he had to sell it or risk losing it. At that same time, the Universal Milking Machine—a primitive precursor to today's sophisticated automated milking systems—was growing in popularity. To stay in the business would have meant renovations to the milkhouse and a great deal of upgrading, so Walter switched over to beef cattle. He retained a smaller crop of chickens for farm gate sales. With quota and the growing automation of farming, specialization—rather than the mixed farms of Walter's youth—had become the norm.

Walter collecting eggs in 1988.

When it came time to retire, Walter passed the farm on to his own son, but he continued to live there—trading the house for a 5th wheel trailer. He and his wife spent the summers parked in the backyard, where they continued to lend a hand when needed. Come the colder weather, they would pack up and head south. After so many years on the farm, they found the best of both worlds carrying their home behind them on their travels.

Scenes from a Stratford Boyhood
Ralph Wagner

Ralph biked down the street, his tires rustling through the fallen autumn leaves in the gutter. He was on his way to the grocery store in Market Square, sent by his mother to pick up a few ingredients for the evening meal. He dropped his bike at the front door and went in for his purchases. As he emerged from the store, he ran into his friend and together they continued down Ontario Street.

"What's going on down there?" he asked, pointing to the crowd growing outside of the Beacon Herald office half a block down Ontario Street. The Beacon always posted the latest headlines scribbled on paper on a bulletin board in their shop window, so passers-by could stay abreast of the news. Whatever was on the bulletin board was causing a commotion. Some people were boisterous, calling out to one another and shaking hands, while others read the board and quickly walked away with drawn faces.

Curious, Ralph and his friend left their bikes and walked over, slipping under elbows and through spaces in the crowd until they were standing in front of the window of the Beacon Herald. In thick block letters, the headline read: CANADA AT WAR WITH NAZIS.

Ralph Wagner was born in a little house across from the library in the year 1929, a few months before the famous stock market crash which brought the world economy to its knees. His father was fortunate to have one of the few jobs which actually prospered as a result of the Depression; he was a travelling shoe cobbler who drove between London and Seaforth in his panel van full of shoe parts and tools. At a time when many people couldn't afford to buy new shoes, his repair supplies and services were in high demand. As a result, the family of six was able to make it through the Depression without much hardship—although there were no luxuries.

Young Ralph on his trike.

The Wagner's backyard was the most popular in the neighbourhood because they were the only family with a swing set. The grass was constantly worn away by little feet running in and out of their yard. A veritable menagerie could also be found there, thanks to Ralph's penchant for rescuing animals from classmates who couldn't keep them anymore. The first pet he brought home was a curly-tailed dog, which the family called a 'Heinz 57 terrier.' They took her on vacation to a trailer they had rented in Bright's Grove. One day while the children were at the beach, the dog escaped and started chasing the neighbour's chickens. Ralph's mother had to trample all over the garden to get him back. The little dog wasn't nearly as troublesome as the two white mice to whom he offered sanctuary next. That quickly got out of hand as those two mice multiplied into thirty-two mice, much to his mother's horror. The last animal he saved was the family favourite—a big friendly collie that had grown up on a farm outside of town.

Ralph's first job was at an egg-grading station on the lot behind the family's house. Farmers brought their eggs in tall stacks of flats to be sorted by size and candled. The process of candling was done to determine how fresh the egg was. By shining a bright light behind the egg's semi-translucent shell, the air bubble inside would be illuminated. If the air bubble was dime-sized, it meant the egg was fresh. After school and all day Saturday, Ralph would feed eggs from the flats onto the scale which sorted them into sizes. He also delivered two paper routes: one for the Beacon Herald and the other for Toronto Star. He did not relish the job in the winter when he had to pick up the stack of Stars at the train station and deliver them across town to Hibernia Street even in the blowing snow and bitter winds.

Ralph as a teenager.

Ralph was in high school during the war, and like all boys, he had to participate in the Cadets program. They would march around the track in the backyard of Stratford Collegiate Vocational Institute, practicing their drills. Due to wartime need, cars were scarce, and only those who depended on them for their professions were able to purchase them. When Ralph's father's van engine developed a knock, he could not replace the vehicle. He simply had to adjust, which meant driving no faster than 30 miles per hour at any time. That made his sales calls to London rather tedious; however, he made do.

At home on Church Street.

Ralph remembers going down to the Avon River with his friends to watch the Mosquito bomber fly overhead. Part of the bomber's wing was being manufactured in Stratford at the time, so there was a demonstration being held to show residents the finished aircraft in action. The airplane made a real impression on him as a young boy, flying low along the length of the river and then disappearing into the blue sky before anyone could blink.

After the war ended, and Ralph finished high school,

he moved away from Stratford, living in cities as far-flung as Sudbury and Santa Barbara, California. He returned to downtown Stratford to operate a stationery store on Ontario Street where H.H. Delea now stands, and afterwards spent many years in Toronto selling cherubic Hummel figurines and giftware. He has now settled down to spend his retirement days in Stratford.

The End of the One-Room Schoolhouse

Dorothy Hart

The sun beat down on the students of S.S. #4 Grey Township. They were lined along the train tracks near the outskirts of Stratford, waiting with as much patience as they could muster. Squinting down the tracks, they could see crowds gathered on either side for some distance. They all leaned forward, hoping to catch the first glimpse of the train. At last, they heard a whistle faintly in the distance, and the children jittered with anticipation. The king and queen were on their way.

Dorothy's day had started early, as she joined her bubbly classmates at the train station in Brussels. Most had never been as far away from home as Stratford, and they were giddy with excitement as their train pulled into the city. They disembarked and followed their teacher to the grassy spot along the rail line which had been designated for their school. The train was supposed to slow as it reached the city limits, ensuring all the spectators would have their chance to wave at the royals as they passed.

Finally, the train chugged into sight. The students crowded closer together as it neared, jostling and straining to see. Then suddenly—WHOOSH—it passed them, offering not even the slightest glimpse of the royals and leaving a crowd of disappointed onlookers in its wake.

Dorothy Hart was born on a farm six miles from Brussels. Her mother had been a schoolteacher, so she always knew that she was expected to go to high school, though she was the only one in her class who did. After completing eighth grade in a one-room schoolhouse, she moved in with her grandparents in town to attend Brussels Continuation School. There were only five classes, one for each grade of high school.

On Sunday evenings, Dorothy's mother would send a care package into town with her, consisting of food and baked goods to last the week. Dorothy's days were spent in the classroom and her evenings at the local general store, where she had a part-time job. On weeknights, she worked until six p.m., but on Saturdays the store stayed open until 10 or 11 p.m. to accommodate farmers from the surrounding area who could only come in to do their weekly shopping after the outdoor work was done. Dorothy's father would pick her up after her shift and bring her home for a visit. At the store, Dorothy earned $8 a week, which she considered to be a very good wage. By the time she finished high school, she had saved enough to pay her way through teachers' college.

Dorothy was accepted into the Normal School, 40 miles away in Stratford. She had only been to Stratford once before, with her public school on the ill-fated trip to see the royals in 1939, so the move was quite an adjustment. Fortunately, her cousin had enrolled in a business school in Stratford, so the two of them set off for the city together. They boarded with a family who lived on the second floor of a garage on Ontario Street. Beneath them, the man of the house operated a taxi business. These taxis were hired by the school board to transport Dorothy and other teaching students to schools across the county for their weekly practice-teaching placements.

Dorothy quickly immersed herself in life at the Normal School. She joined the glee club, which practiced and performed music at special occasions. Every month, the Normal School held an afternoon program of musical and dramatic performances by the students. Their purpose extended beyond entertainment; they also taught students how to go about organizing musical events. When they were placed in classrooms of their own, their experience with these shows made the task of organizing the all-important Christmas concert much less daunting. The glee club's big performance was at the At Home dance in the spring before graduation, where they performed songs from the musical *Oklahoma!*

The Normal School graduation ceremonies.

Facing her first classroom of children at the age of nineteen, Dorothy reports having "butterflies galore." She taught grades one through four at Hampstead School, north of Stratford. The community there was warm and welcoming, and before long, Dorothy began a courtship with a local farmer. After three years of teaching, she married and settled into her new role as a farmer's wife and mother. In the 1950s, women rarely taught after they were married. Dorothy never imagined that she would be back at the front of the classroom.

Dorothy, in her second year of teaching at Hampstead.

This changed after an unexpected visit one March afternoon several years later. By then, Dorothy had four young children and was living on the Hart homestead with her husband and his parents. It was after lunch, and the men were out in the fields, so Dorothy was the only one at home when three men came knocking at the door. They were the trustees for a school in Ellice Township.

She invited them in, and they explained their dilemma. The current teacher at their school was not working out, and they were desperate for someone to replace her after the Easter break. They asked if she would do it. "I wouldn't dream of it!" she replied. Raising four young kids and managing a busy household did not leave any extra time for the demanding job of a teacher. That evening at dinner when she recounted the story of their visit, nobody said much. Afterwards, Dorothy was in the kitchen finishing the supper dishes when her father-in-law came to her and said, "Dorothy, if you want to teach, Ma and I will keep the kids."

All of a sudden, she began to consider the offer more seriously. After much deliberation, she decided to give it a try, just for a year. From Easter until the summer vacation, her husband's parents tended the children during the day while she returned to the classroom. Since she didn't drive, her father-in-law took her to school each morning and brought her home at night. When school ended for the summer, everyone agreed that it was time for her to learn to drive herself. In the fall, they hired a local girl to care for the children, and Dorothy returned to her classroom. With those adjustments, the experiment worked—Dorothy continued to teach for another 22 years.

Baseball at recess.

In the mid-1960s, plans began to surface for a central school that would collect students from all of the tiny one-room schoolhouses across North Easthope Township. Dorothy was offered a position in advance of its grand opening, which was slated for September 1966. However, the building's completion was delayed until the following January. The teachers worked hard to coordinate their curriculum so the students would be at the same level when they were united in January. In an effort to create classrooms in advance, all the students across the township in a certain grade were transported by bus to one of the small schools. Finally, the doors opened, and students filled the shining halls, spacious classrooms, and bright new gymnasium.

For Dorothy, the first day of school at North Easthope Public was the most nerve-wracking of them all. For her entire career, she was used to being alone in a rural classroom, with just her and the children. The only other person she expected to see was the school inspector, who visited twice yearly. Now, the next teacher was a few steps down the hall; her voice could be heard through the walls! Dorothy was accustomed to handling 30 pupils; at North Easthope, there were over 300 pupils in total. However, she soon grew to enjoy the new arrangement and relished the chance to delve more deeply into the subject matter with only one grade to worry about. After a 25 year career, Dorothy retired to the farm, now an integral part of the same community which had welcomed her fresh out of teacher's college.

A Tale of Many Mountains
Margaret Erb

*Margaret looked over her shoulder as the Swiss
Alps disappeared behind her. Below the white-tipped
peaks, she could see several pastoral villages and
cow sheds nestled among the slopes. She had been
born in one of those small villages, where her father worked as a blacksmith. By day, he worked
with steel and anvil, but by night he dreamed of
farming.*

*Now, the family was bound for the wide open
spaces of Canada to fulfill these ambitions. Their
train carried them through the French country-
side, ravaged and devastated by the recent war.
Once in England, they boarded The Empress of
Canada, and set off across the ocean for Canada.
Though the Swiss mountains were behind them,
Margaret's journeys were only just beginning.*

In the evenings when she was a child, Margaret Erb's father would pore over books about farming. He had followed
in his father's footsteps to become a blacksmith by trade,
but his true interest was in working the land. He kept the
blacksmith shop in Oberwangen, a little village outside the
capital Bern, until his mother passed away. After that, the
family became caretakers of a schoolhouse in a nearby town.
In the late thirties, Margaret's father left for Argentina, in
search of a farm to buy. Her mother remained in Switzerland with the children who helped out with the cleaning and
grounds-keeping at the school. There were no phones at the
time, so they would watch closely for the mail, anxious to
hear news from South America.

Finally, they received a very exciting letter. Margaret's father had found the perfect farm in Argentina! He wrote glowing descriptions of the landscape and climate, telling the children that they would have to learn to use a lasso to rope the calves. However, before the family could fulfill their plans to join him, a locust swarm devastated the area. All that was left were barren fields, no longer a farm fit for anyone to purchase. Meanwhile, the news reports from Europe grew more and more frightening, and war seemed imminent. Margaret's father caught a boat back to Switzerland, arriving home shortly before the first shots of the Second World War echoed across the continent.

He didn't give up on the dream of farming. After more research, he decided that Canada was the frontier he was looking for. By then, Margaret had moved to work in the French area of Switzerland as an *au pair*. In 1948, she received a call from her father, telling her to hurry home—the ship was departing in three weeks. With hardly any time to bid her friends goodbye, Margaret packed her belongings and set off, along with her parents, her sister, and two brothers. All they knew of Canada was that there were skunks there.

Their journey through France was eye-opening and heartbreaking. While the family had experienced the strain of rationing during the war, their small village had remained fairly insulated from the horrors of the battlefield. They could not have imagined the destruction and devastation that was passing before their eyes as they gazed out of the train window. They stopped for a day in London, which was also struggling to rebuild from the wreckage that the bombs had left behind.

In the port city of Liverpool, they could at last board their boat. The family had bought passage in steerage, so their rooms were in the bottom of the hold with no windows. They could only go on deck at certain hours, when the higher-paying passengers would not be out. This didn't matter much because everyone was sick except for Margaret's father. Margaret's mother didn't make it to the deck at all during the entire voyage. Margaret spent most of the trip caring for her eleven-month-old sibling.

Everyone was relieved when they finally landed in Montreal. Margaret stood on deck and watched as her father's huge, beautifully-carved wooden trunk was lowered onto land in a big net with the other luggage. From the boat, the family piled onto a train bound west. Margaret was proud to be able to use the French she had learned as an *au pair* to converse with some Quebecois men they met along the way. After their long journey, the family finally arrived in Seaforth, their new home. At last, her father had the farm he had longed for.

Though her father's stint as a farmer did not prove to be fruitful, Margaret remained a rural girl after her marriage. She and her husband Harold operated a large apple orchard, which kept them very busy for over thirty years. It wasn't until the family moved into Stratford that her travelling instincts returned, through service trips upon which she and her husband embarked.

After visits to Dominica and Haiti, Margaret and Harold were sent to a remote area of Papua New Guinea which had not experienced outside contact until the 1960s. A gold mining company had discovered a very profitable mining site and was in the process of building roads through the rainforest. No roads reached the village where the Erbs went, which was surrounded on all four sides by lush mountains.

Margaret marvelled at the native Papua New Guinean's ability to walk easily on the steep slopes, bringing fresh food down the mountains in billums, cloth bags which hung from their foreheads. They would trade their produce for fish and rice at the store the Erbs operated. The store didn't last long, because the locals were very clever at extracting more goods than they had bargained for. Sometimes they would bring in 20 lbs. of potatoes, sneak them out the back door, and return with the same 20 lbs. for more trading.

A market scene in Papua New Guinea.

After several other service endeavors, the Erbs decided to go to Belize to meet with locals and find out how they could help. They bought a van and drove for nine days through the United States, down along the Gulf of Mexico, and finally into Belize City. There, they found there was a need for gestetners, a forerunner of the photocopier which was operated by a hand crank. They collected these, along with ink and paper, and brought them to several schools in the area, where they were used to make copies of everything from graduation certificates to school exams. At each school they visited, Margaret would spend time reading to the children, since Belize is an English-speaking country.

Several years after they had returned to Stratford, many local churches were throwing away their gestetners, present-

Delivering books in Belize.

ing an opportunity that was too good to pass up. Harold and Margaret bought a huge Much Music van which they refurbished into a bedroom for themselves, and filled a 40-foot trailer with gestetners as well as books, clothes, and equipment. Their second journey to Belize was fraught with challenges, as the van seemed to break down at every turn. However, they met kind people at each juncture who were willing to lend a hand—sometimes offering a spare part or their mechanical expertise, other times letting the Erbs stay with them as the van was repaired. Most nights, they would park at gas stations to sleep, although the noise of the trucks coming and going made that nearly impossible at times.

After a nail-biting journey through a mountainous region of Mexico in which the van had to struggle to crest each hill, the axle of the trailer bent. The Erbs were fortunate to meet an English-speaking local who put them up for three days while the trailer was being fixed. During that time, both Harold and their host had a birthday, so Margaret bought a piñata and filled it with goodies for the two to celebrate with. At each stop on that tumultuous trip, they found that good fortune followed, no matter how bleak it seemed.

After twenty-two days on the road, Margaret and Harold were relieved to finally reach their destination and begin distributing the goods. In the years since, they have spent more time in Stratford and less time travelling—but they take joy in the knowledge that they made a difference, in some small way.

Sights Set
Bruce Shivas

Bruce woke with a start and looked around him. In the darkened room, he could see the other members of his regiment sleeping, apparently undisturbed. They were stationed in an empty school in Nijmegen, a city in eastern Netherlands near the border with Germany. The school was only a snowball's throw away from the Rhine, which was regularly trawled by German submarines seeking to blow out the bridge. There was a gasworks across the road, which had to be patched constantly with wet sandbags as it was punctured by shells. The men kept their helmets on at all times, even inside.

Bruce noticed that the floor around him was scattered with debris. Still, nothing seemed seriously amiss. Finally, he looked up, and found himself staring straight at an 88 mm shell. It had blown through the roof, through a 2 by 10 inch plank, and ended up wedged in the ceiling. It hung suspended there over top of him, unexploded. Bruce knew that Germans had recruited people in occupied territories to work in munitions factories, and occasionally when the foreman wasn't looking, they would neglect to put the fuse in the bomb. In this case, the bomb hanging over his head had no fuse, so it didn't go off.

There in the classroom, Bruce breathed a silent thank you to that munitions factory worker who had almost certainly saved his life that day.

Bruce Shivas had already been doing war work for several years as a tool and dye maker in Stratford when he enlisted for the army at age 21. He completed his basic training in Listowel and advanced training in Calgary, followed by one year of mechanical training in Hamilton. They learned to sharpen drills and do machine work without a machine shop, because they would be working with limited resources overseas. His technical training was completed in Kingston. Every weekend, he took the train back to Stratford, studying on the way there and back. Then, the time came to bid his family farewell and leave for England.

It was November when he left, and the seas were rough. Bruce spent much of the trip in the centre of the ship because it was pitching too much to stand at either end. It was a relief to be on solid ground again after the harrowing crossing, and he got straight to work. He was placed with the 6th Light Anti-Aircraft Regiment and quickly became overrun with work repairing binoculars. The binoculars were used by anti-aircraft gunners who were stationed in southern England and tasked with shooting down enemy planes in the skies above. It was imperative that their binoculars were sighted perfectly, because they had to be sure the planes they were targeting were indeed the enemy.

Headquarters sent Bruce across England, visiting each anti-aircraft unit in turn. After a few missed connections, he quickly learned to navigate the complicated train system. It didn't take long for him to realize that the task was bigger than he could handle alone; many of the binoculars in use were borrowed from English noblemen or left over from the First World War, and they were in terrible shape. "I told headquarters that I needed help, unless they expected the war to go on for another four or five years," he recalls. He got a team, and together they were able to keep the binoculars sighted, sealed, and in top shape.

A few days after the D-Day invasion began, Bruce trav-

Bruce in England.

elled with his regiment across the channel. They suited their vehicles up with waterproof covers and boarded an English boat. This took them most of the way across, but when they got closer to the shore, they and their vehicles had to be transferred by crane to a smaller boat. When it was Bruce's turn, they picked up the Jeep he was driving and lowered him down. He was nearly settled on the smaller boat when somebody yelled, "Tea!" Never one to miss their teatime, the Englishmen running the crane took a break, leaving Bruce suspended in his Jeep just above the smaller boat.

There he hung, waiting for what felt like a very long time. The smaller boat rose and rocked, causing it to bang against the bottom of the Jeep with every wave. Finally, the crane operators returned, and he was set down. When they got close enough to see the shore, the boat could take them no further. In their waterproofed vehicles, they drove through the water up onto the beach. Higher on the hills, there were

German soldiers shooting from hidden locations. The front line could be seen in the distance. It was a tense landing, but they finally made it to a protected area.

Once in France, Bruce moved with his regiment, going out to do repairs by day and then returning at night to sleep. He became accustomed to sleeping outside, even in December. Each night, he would dig out a hollow to hang his hammock in, drive the truck over top, and crawl in to sleep amidst the rattle of the shells. It was the only way to stay dry. However, even that strategy ran afoul when he found himself in a low spot, and the hole filled up with water. On those occasions, he would wake up completely wet with no hope of drying off. At times they were only a half-mile away from the fighting, and the noise of the guns was constant. They began to adjust to taking life day by day, getting through their agenda for today and worrying about tomorrow when it came.

As they made their way through northern Holland, it became evident that the war had taken a toll on the civilians there. When the regiment stopped in villages for lunch, Bruce would take any coffee that was left over in the pot and go door-to-door down the street, pouring cups at each house. The Dutch people hadn't had coffee for years. Another thing that had grown very scarce over the course of the war was fabric. Women had to resort to collecting used parachutes to make clothes for their families. Once, Bruce's pyjama bottoms were stolen right off the laundry line of the home where he was billeted. He had to do some negotiating to get a new pair.

Bruce's brother was also serving in Holland, where he boarded with an elderly woman. She had a hard time buying underwear due to the fabric shortage, so Bruce's brother sent a note home asking for his mother to send a pair in the right size. During wartime, it was illegal to ship new goods through the mail, so Bruce's mother put the underwear on over her clothes for five minutes—just long enough to qualify them as 'used'—before sending them. Bruce's brother gave them to the woman with whom he was staying, and he reported that she was "tickled pink." In this way, the Dutch people and their Allied liberators helped each other along.

One morning in May, Bruce got word that the war would officially end at noon. Anticipation grew as the noon hour approached. Then, only a few hours before the war was over for good, he watched as a Canadian soldier crossing the street was hit by a German bullet and fell. It was hard to feel jubilant, despite the relief that VE Day brought. In the coming months, not much changed in day-to-day life. The guns had stopped firing, but there were still land mines and other hazards hidden in the landscape. Bruce remained in northern Holland, collecting, cleaning, and repairing all the binoculars that had been used during the war in preparation for future conflicts should they arise. His return was further delayed by a lengthy hospital stay while he recovered from pleurisy with effusion and tuberculosis.

At last, Bruce returned to Stratford and to his tool and dye trade. Though his war service is now far behind him, he has remained a 'fixer' for his whole life. Even after retiring as president and general manager of Perth Metal Industries, he continued to take on various projects. He is well known for his creative eye, his precise workmanship, and his eagerness to put his hands to work fixing things.

"Number, please. . ."
Betty Larkworthy

The sky over Stratford was dark and threatening as Betty walked in the door of the Bell Telephone Company, reporting for her shift as operator there. "Oh my," she thought to herself. "It's going to be a busy one."

Inside, 29 women were hard at work, 15 covering local calls and 14 assigned to long distance. "Number please," they began, and the person on the line would respond with the number they wanted to reach. "Thank you," the operators replied, taking the key from the back panel and placing it in the corresponding front panel. Each telephone call made in the Stratford area came through them, and the lines were always especially busy around weather changes as people cancelled plans, called for rides, and stayed in to chat instead of going out.

Betty assumed her position at the switchboard. "Number please," she said clearly.

"Did we get you away from your magazine?" the voice on the other end replied sarcastically. Betty shook her head dismissively. A little mild abuse was part of the job. As the rain began to patter on the sidewalk outside, she connected the first of hundreds of phone calls that shift.

Betty Larkworthy's childhood was spread across various southern Ontario towns, each connected by the CNR tracks. Her father was a telegrapher with CNR, and during the Depression he moved many times, thanks to a CNR policy which allowed workers to take the jobs of others with less seniority upon losing their own positions. They started out in Exeter, but when a position was cut at that station, the family moved to Guelph Junction. After three years, another position was cut there, sending them on to Wingham. There, one of her father's responsibilities was to send the news between London and Wingham newspapers. In those days, the wire was the fastest way to transport news, so he was busy from four until midnight—often working overtime when the newsmen were late in their delivery. The job was tedious, so when a position came up in the main depot of Guelph, he was glad to take it. Betty's parents had "a wonderful capacity for welcoming people," so no matter what town they were in, their home was always a pleasant place.

In Guelph, Betty finished high school and got a job as an operator at the Bell Telephone Company at a starting wage of $7 per week. After three years, her father received his last transfer, to Stratford, where he was the dispatcher. As far as her father was concerned, this was "the top." His role—phoning in the train orders between Kincardine and Stratford, and Stratford and Toronto—was an important one. When Betty was transferred to the Bell office in Stratford six months later, she quickly grew fond of the city.

The Bell was a wonderful place to work at that time. Though the workers had no union, Bell had their own way of keeping things even between workers. Since the phones needed to be open 24 hours, everyone had to take their turn on night shifts. Day shifts between 8 a.m. and 6 p.m. lasted eight hours. The "split trick" shift, which was three hours in the morning and four hours at night, lasted for seven hours. Those working the late shift from 6 p.m. until midnight had only a six-hour shift. Anyone finishing work after 11 p.m. was taken home by taxi. The cab company employed three brothers, each of whom coincidentally married a Bell Telephone girl.

Working at the Bell had other perks as well. The company would take their workers on outings and to different courses as far away as Toronto. After the course, they would be treated to dinner in a fine restaurant. The best part, however, was the camaraderie between the women. Though they had their spats, they truly felt like a family, all working for "Mother Bell."

The telephone lines became especially busy when the Stratford Festival began in 1953. The night operators got most of the calls from reporters who wanted to know more about the small city and their brand-new festival. Betty was in the audience of the very first production, *Richard III*. Like many townspeople, she threw her support behind the fledgling festival. She helped to serve at the dinners that were held for the actors at Knox Church. Many of them were young and poor, so the community put together full-course meals for only a dollar throughout the season. Betty was mortified when she accidentally spilled coffee on the actor Don Greenall at one such dinner. Betty also volunteered at the information kiosk downtown and worked in the box office. At that time, people ordered their tickets by mail, and Betty and her co-workers sent them the tickets for the seats they requested in return.

One day, Betty's father returned from an appointment with the new optometrist in town with a message. "Dr. Larkworthy says it's about time for you to come in and have your eyes examined," he said. She did, and afterwards they went out for coffee. Sparks flew from the first appointment onwards. Before long, they married and moved into a home on Ontario Street where they raised their daughter. Betty's husband had been a bomber pilot during the war so he was used to being in charge, but she could hold her own.

Over the years, tourism in Stratford increased, as did Betty's involvement with it. She led downtown heritage tours and step-on coach bus tours, becoming well-versed in the

city's history. Through her connection to the Stratford archives, Betty became very interested in the architecture of different Stratford houses.

One summer, she and her dog walked the entire city with
the architectural guide in hand, looking at different styles
of homes and studying their distinctive features. She began
to devote her energy to restoring her own home on Ontario
Street, which was built in 1926 and exhibits elements of Ed-
wardian Classical and Tudor Revival, with a transition to
Prairie style. Re-painting, re-furbishing, and refinishing every aspect of the home with careful attention to historical
accuracy was a terrific amount of work, but Betty truly enjoyed the process. From its coffered ceilings to its period-
correct light fixtures, the house is her masterpiece, achieving
a heritage designation in 1998.

The Winding Nith
Mildred Rupert

The little girl with her hair in two long braids sat at the school desk, her feet barely brushing the floor. The older boys and girls were taking spelling dictation, their graphite squeaking against the slate as they wrote. At the front, the teacher read out the words slowly, repeating them three times, but the little girl paid no attention. She was staring at the Little Red Hen Reader which was open in front of her. All of a sudden, she was struck by a realization.

"I can read that!" she thought to herself. It was the strangest sensation she had ever felt.

One day, she would go on to write a book of her own.

Born on a 200 acre farm in Wellesley Township, Mildred Rupert grew up with an intimate knowledge of the rhythm of the farming seasons. The spring began with birdsong and crocuses pushing their heads through the melting snowdrifts. The warmer temperatures meant it was time to tap the maple trees in the sugar bush. They collected sap from 100 trees, boiling and straining it first outside in a cauldron over the fire, and then again on the kitchen stove until it thickened. There was always enough to last the year, and some left over to sell.

When the ground thawed and puddles dried up, days were filled with cultivating, ploughing, and seeding. As a child, Mildred enjoyed walking behind the team of horses as they pulled the plough. They used no pesticides, so hoeing

Mildred and her son George.

their ten-acre cornfield was a time-consuming and constant chore. There was also the potato patch to tend, crawling with red striped bugs that needed to be picked off before they devoured the entire plant. In the summer, the women spent much of their time between the garden and the kitchen, planting, weeding, and picking the vegetables that they preserved for the winter. Their cellar shelves would bend under the weight of the jars. Jams, jellies, chili sauce, relish, ketchup, and canned fruits of every description waited in the cool darkness to be eaten when the snow fell again.

There was always field work to keep Mildred and her five siblings busy, especially in the late summer when they would spend days stooking the oats, barley, and wheat. Her favourite time of the year was the fall, after the harvest was taken in. Then, there was a chance to relax and enjoy the last of the sunshine before winter's arrival.

When she married, Mildred moved to her husband's family farm one block away from the hamlet of Nithburg. The

Nith River meandered through their lower field, flanked on either side by willow trees. It crossed under a bridge at the base of their farm, before flowing on towards Wellesley.

The old bridge over the Nith River.

One September several years after she had moved there, construction crews came to rebuild the bridge. At the end of the week, they left their building materials on the flat field alongside the river. That Saturday night, there was a heavy rainstorm which swelled the normally slow-moving river far beyond its banks. Mildred looked out the window the next morning to see the construction materials floating away as the water poured downstream. Her husband notified the construction site manager, who hurried over after church with his son and his son's friend.

Mildred was on the party line phone with her neighbour marvelling at the height of the river when their conversation was interrupted. It was the site manager, calling from the phone down at the bridge. In a tight voice, he told Mildred that needed to make a call right away. When her husband came in from the barn after gathering the eggs, Mildred sent him down to figure out what had transpired. Returning hours later, he carried sombre news. While trying to salvage some of the wood, one of the young men had been swept away by the swift current. His body hadn't yet been recovered.

For the next several days, the river was traversed again and again by rescue workers, police, neighbours, and community members. An orange helicopter swooped overhead, searching. However, none of their efforts prevailed in retrieving the young man. Discouraged, a group of neighbours decided to pay a visit to Vera McNichol in Millbank. Vera was a local celebrity of sorts—her fortune-telling skills were widely sought-after, not only in the township but around the world. She kept no appointment book, so the only way to solicit her advice was to come directly to her Millbank home and wait amidst the others who lined the driveway hoping for an audience. She welcomed visitors into her kitchen and charged no fees for her services.

During their visit, Vera prophesied that the body would be found after the water went down, in a wash-out on the flats. The following Wednesday dawned a sunny day, and Mildred looked out her window again to see that the river had finally sunk within its banks. That afternoon, searchers found the body just where Vera had predicted, in a wash-out in the field. He was only eighteen years old when he died. It was difficult to look at the river, normally so peaceful and gentle, in the same way after that.

Mildred's husband had served for many years as the assessor for the township of North Easthope. Travelling to each farm in the township annually, he got to know the community very well. They had often agreed that someone ought to write a history of Nithburg. Many years later, Mildred and two other Nithburg women decided to put one together. After some planning over an afternoon tea, Mildred and her friend Miriam Zettel began to collect information. They talked to Nithburg residents about their memories, they gathered old photographs, and they traced the history of the small village back to its first residents. Soon they had amassed a great deal of information, from personal accounts to historical records. Unsure how to proceed, they gave their collection to Rowena Gerber, another Nithburg woman who stepped up to edit, compile, and publish the book.

She stopped in at Mildred's house one afternoon, carrying a big cardboard box. Setting it on the kitchen table, she pulled out a copy of their book, a complete history of the town of Nithburg! All 400 copies sold.

Mildred's husband Lorne in 1950.

It Started in the Sandbox

Donna Lee

The afternoon sun was warming the backyard where two little girls played in a sand box. Their faces were etched with concentration as they patted and pushed the sand into castles and towers. Sand curled beneath their feet and found its way into the folds and ruffles of their dresses as they played. It was a picture of contentment.

A neighbour came along and stood over them, casting a long shadow across the sandbox.

"You're getting your dress dirty," she said with a scolding tone.

Donna looked across at her friend, and up at the neighbour. "That's okay," she said with youthful wisdom. "My mother has a washing machine."

Donna Lee and her best friend Shirley grew up in houses right beside each other in 1930s Peterborough. Their first meeting was in the sandbox, and they soon became inseperable. Climbing trees, dressing up their dolls, and playing make-believe occupied their early years. Together with the other neighbourhood kids, they would play outside until the streetlights came on, signalling that it was bedtime.

When Shirley went to kindergarten, she took Donna along, even though Donna was one year too young. Shirley also took Donna to church each Sunday because the Anglican church was just around the corner, while the Baptist church that Donna's parents attended was a long way across town. They skipped grade six together, and their adventures continued into the first year of high school. It was in grade nine that Donna went on her first date—a double date to the movies with Shirley and two boys from Lakefield College School, a private boarding school not far from Peterborough. One afternoon they decided to bike out to the prestigious school to visit. They were allowed to stay for dinner in the formal dining hall, but much to their chagrin they had to sit at the head table with all the teachers.

Though Donna was only twelve when she began high school, that didn't stop her from getting involved. Because it was wartime, nearly all the school activities were aimed at raising funds for the war effort, which was consuming the resources of the entire country. In her last year, Donna was active on the committee organizing the year-end formal dance. It was a splashy affair. The great excitement was the musical act, Shirley Harmer. She was a well-known jazz singer who could often be heard on the CBC Radio in the evenings.

The day of the dance dawned grey and threatening and before long a dreadful blizzard had buried the city in snowdrifts. It looked as if all their planning would go to waste. However, in spite of Donna's worries, the bus carrying the band got through the storm. The dance went smoothly, although the same could not be said for Donna's drive home that evening. At every corner, the car floundered and slipped into another snowdrift. Each time they had to get out and push the car. She didn't get to bed until five in the morning. Bright and early the next day, she reported to a local department store for her first shift. According to Donna, "I was so tired I couldn't add two and two together." Nevertheless, they kept her on.

At eighteen, Donna married her high school sweetheart. Her mother made her wedding dress, and they held the reception in their home. Afterwards, they drove up and down Main Street in their friend's Model T Ford, honking the horn while streamers fluttered out behind them.

The young couple moved to Toronto, where Donna's husband Ernie had a job in a bank. It was shortly after the war, and housing was nearly impossible to find. The flat that they eventually rented consisted of only two rooms and a bathroom. There was no sink in the kitchen (which was also their living room), so she had to haul water in each time she washed dishes.

Cooking was a challenge in those early years as well. There was a hotplate with only two burners. "You could either have the stove going, or the oven going, take your choice!" she recalls. To make matters worse, Donna was the youngest child, and her mother had taught the older two sisters to cook but not Donna. She learned the basics from Ernie and went on to become a wonderful cook. They didn't mind the cramped conditions; they were so happy to be together, with no parents to tell them what to do. In 1950, they welcomed a son, followed by another daughter and son in subsequent years.

Long after the children were in bed, Donna could often be found bent over her sewing machine, re-making their clothes so they would have new dresses and suits to wear. Her motivation for learning to sew stemmed from the frustration of never being able to find a jacket and skirt set that would fit. Taking matters into her own hands, Donna bought a pattern and made her own. This was the first of many successful sewing projects. Before long, she was making all of her own clothes. Donna expanded upon her skills by taking courses in tailoring and millinery pattern making.

With the frequent moves that accompanied being a banker's wife, Donna grew adept at adapting to new homes and new faces. In every new place she met kind people—and stayed in touch with special friends from the past, including her childhood companion Shirley. Though their sandbox days are far behind them, they still keep in touch.

Neighbours in North Easthope
Ivan and Mynetta Stueck

It was a cold January day, and across the countryside, children were pulling out their rusty ice skates or their long wooden toboggans and tromping through the deep snow for some winter fun. By age fifteen, Ivan had left those carefree days behind him, taking over the brunt of the farm work while his father was sick in bed.

For weeks, the pigs had been weighing heavily on his mind. It was the time of year that they needed to be butchered, but Ivan couldn't do it himself. Fortunately, in a farming community, one never truly faced his work alone. Hitching up the cutter and backing it towards their pen, Ivan loaded up the pigs and hauled them to a neighbour's farm through the snow. A few days later, he would return to pick up the pork that they had butchered for him, one of the many favours that were traded back and forth between neighbours.

Ivan and Mynetta Stueck were both born on farms in North Easthope Township. They met in church as youngsters and attended the same one-room schoolhouse. When Ivan was ten, his family bought the farm next to Mynetta's, so they were neighbours for many years. Despite their long acquaintance, their courtship took time to develop, and they didn't marry until they were both thirty years old.

Both have similar memories of growing up on the farm. Their early childhood in the 1920s was prosperous, but the Depression brought challenges to all farmers. Suddenly, the

105

prices for farm products plummeted to next to nothing. In the '20s, it wouldn't be unreasonable to expect a market pig to sell for $50—by the 30s, they were lucky to fetch $3. Hired men were paid 75 cents a day before the stock market crash, and by 1935, their wage had dropped to 25 cents a day. Times were especially difficult because Ivan's family moved to a larger farm in 1932, requiring them to take out a loan from the bank. Through scrimping and saving, they were able to avoid repossession, which was the fate of many farmers during those times. They had just paid off their farm when Ivan's father grew seriously ill in 1935. After this, Ivan had to take on many of the farming responsibilities himself.

Growing up, Ivan recalls that the worst job on the farm was barn threshing. He would spend ten hours in the den (part of the barn which was open from the floor to the rafters). Tramping straw was the most unpleasant part because it was so dusty. Though it was hot and sweaty in the barn, the air outside was cold by the late autumn. Often, they would get sick with thresh fever afterwards and spend the day in bed chilled and congested as a result of all the dust. Mynetta's family had a steam thresher for as long as she could remember, so she was spared that onerous task. However, she recalls spending a lot of time hoeing.

Butchering was another annual job that was done at home, usually in the cold weather after the New Year. Mynetta's father was an accomplished butcher, so he would travel to his neighbour's farms to help them with their butchering. He knew the proper ingredients and preservatives to add when making the sausage and the best methods for preserving the meat.

Usually each family would butcher three or four hogs a year. Some of it would be packed in snow and ice to remain frozen for the winter months, but most of it was cured. After spending ten to twelve days in the smokehouse, the meat would last for the rest of the year without spoiling. The women would can frying sausage with a little bit of lard, and the heady smell of summer sausage would fill the cold cellar where they hung. Before the days of refrigeration, the only access that farmers had to a freezer was in the general store in Wellesley. There was a big freezer room attached to the store which was divided into many compartments. Each farmer could rent a locker for a year, where they could store some of their meat and frozen goods, even in the heat of summertime.

With the advent of the war, farming became profitable again as huge markets opened up in Britain. Soon, farmers were sending pork and beef across the ocean, and prices escalated quickly, fuelling improvements and innovations on the farm. Ivan and Mynetta both recall when their houses were first illuminated by electricity. Suddenly, their home was presented in an entirely new perspective, and they didn't always like what they saw. Every corner was suddenly thrust into the spotlight; what had looked quaint by lamplight looked shabby in the glaring electric lights. Despite this, electricity made things easier in countless ways.

Through all the changes that have occurred through their lifetime, one thing has remained constant for the Stuecks: their commitment to the church community. They grew up in a time when church was the first priority. Saturdays were spent preparing the Sunday meal, which would be enjoyed with family or neighbours after the church service. There were always Sunday school classes and Young People's group meetings to attend, as well as various church socials. Though they now live in Stratford, they continue to attend the red brick St. James Lutheran Church in North Easthope, only a block away from the farm where they lived together for 52 years.

Ivan and Mynetta on the day of their farm sale.

The World by the Tail
Don McCaul

Don whistled as the doors of Stratford Collegiate Vocational Institute swung shut behind him. It was the last day of school, and he looked forward to the summer months of freedom that stretched ahead of him. He started for the path down the hill when the caretaker of the school called out to him.

"How'd you like a job?" he asked.

"Well, what is it?" Don asked.

"I need someone to mow the lawn," the caretaker replied. "I'll pay you 35 cents an hour."

Don surveyed the wide lawn, which stretched all the way down the hill towards the river, then looked at the lawnmower which the caretaker was leaning on. Its rusty metal blades spun at the base of a wooden handle. The sun was hot overhead, but the lure of such a generous wage was too strong to resist.

"Sure," he said, taking the lawnmower by the handle. For the next ten hours, he sweated and strained while the hand-mower ground through the grass, cutting narrow swathes through the field until the entire lawn was neatly cut.

In 1923, Don McCaul's father took a job as production manager at McLagan's furniture factory. The family packed up and moved to Stratford, enrolling eight-year-old Don in Falstaff School. His school days were full of amusement. On sunny days, the boys of Falstaff would send a letter to the boys at Avon Public, asking them to join them for a baseball game that night. In the winter, they would gather up their pocket change to rent the rink and play some pick-up hockey. In the spring, each student was given a small plot of land on the school grounds to plant a garden. They were taught to make frames to support the climbing beans and tomatoes, and they carefully dropped the seeds in the ground and watered them faithfully through May and June. When summer holidays came, students were only too happy to banish all thought of school, and as a result, their vegetables grew ripe in the schoolyard with nobody to harvest them.

Don's first job was helping a farmer at the Saturday morning market. The farmer sold potatoes, and Don would drive the horses around delivering the 5 lb. bags to customers. One of the horses was afraid of cars and the other was afraid of people, so it was no easy feat to direct them peacefully down the streets of Stratford. For an afternoon of work, he would be paid a quarter.

In high school, Don continued to work as a delivery boy, this time with Dominion Grocery Store. It stayed open until 11 p.m. on Saturday nights, and he received ten cents for every grocery delivery he made. This time, he had no horse-drawn cart, nor even a bicycle. He simply loaded the groceries into a wagon and delivered the groceries by foot to their intended recipient.

Don graduated from high school in the 1930s, a time when work was hard to find. Stratford was full of men searching for employment, with more arriving by train every day. He took odd jobs at 18 cents an hour, hoping to get into the CNR shops. "Every time you thought you were going to get a job, they decided they needed another baseball player on staff to play for the CNR team," Don jokes. Frustrated, he headed to Toronto where he finally found work in the office of a glass and mirror company. Making $12 a week, he thought he had "the world by the tail." He paid $3 a week for his room at the YMCA and could purchase a full-course meal for 25 cents—35 if you added dessert.

When the war began, Don became involved in the aircraft industry. His headquarters were in Malton, Ontario at Victory Aircraft. This factory later became A.V. Roe and gained fame as the manufacturer of the Avro Arrow. In those days, there were no calculators, and everything was done with pen and paper. Don was sent to aircraft factories in various locations, even travelling all the way to Baltimore, Maryland, to a plant where they were making Martin bombers, a U.S.-designed light bomber. The heat there was so intense that workers were given salt tablets to keep hydrated. Don was surprised to witness segregation on buses and even at drinking fountains.

Many of the factory employees would stop at the same restaurant for breakfast on their way to work in the morning. One day in December 1941, Don arrived at breakfast to find the whole restaurant up in arms. News had just broken about the Japanese attack on Pearl Harbour. This was followed soon after by a formal American declaration of war against Japan, officially bringing the U.S. into World War II. When Don's work in Maryland was nearly finished, he took a train to New York for the weekend to watch a performance by the high-kicking cabaret troupe, the Ziegfeld Follies.

Don returned to Stratford while the war was still on to work at Kroehler's Furniture factory, which was then manufacturing spars for the Mosquito bomber. He had a chance to ride in the Lancaster bomber over Stratford during a patriotic demonstration, "just for show and to get your picture in the paper." He reports that it was not a very comfortable ride; they sat on boxes because there were no seats. After the war, Don stayed on at Kroehler's for another 25 years before deciding that a career change was in order. Undeterred by the fact that he was "older than the teacher," he attended Ryerson to become a public health inspector, a job which he conducted in the Stratford area until his retirement. He also served as chairman of the school board and was instrumental in the building of Northwestern High School.

A Banker's Life

Ernie Lee

Ernie stepped back and surveyed his work. The clapboard church in front of him gleamed under a coat of fresh white paint. Nearly blinding in the autumn sun, the exterior was smooth and perfect. Re-painting the tired old church had been his project all summer. Each evening, he exchanged his suit and tie for a pair of painting overalls and headed to the church, buckets and brushes in hand. He primed, and painted the weathered boards with even brush strokes until sunset, toiling with one goal in mind—to buy a camera.

For years afterwards, he could be found behind the lens of his hard-earned camera, capturing his children's Christmas morning glee, their summer adventures, and their sweet smiles as they grew up.

Ernst Lee was born in 1927 on a eight-acre property outside of Peterborough. His family kept a cow, a horse, and a few chickens while also operating a market garden. Summers were always busy planting, harvesting, and preparing food for the market. When Ernie grew old enough, it was his job to drive the horse and wagon through the streets, delivering produce to the residents of south Peterborough. Back then, three bunches of carrots would cost you a nickel. The family's ample gardens also helped them through the Depression years. They bartered with the local grocer, exchanging potatoes for the grocery staples they couldn't grow themselves.

Ernie was an active student. He took singing and piano lessons throughout public school and often performed solos in his church. This continued into high school, where he was a bugler in the Bugle Band. Like all teenage boys during the war, he received preliminary military training with the Air Cadets. An avid basketball and football player, he was Head Boy in his last year of high school. At the time, there were no school buses, so every morning he would board the city bus into town. One of the girls on the route caught his eye, and he began to save a seat for her each morning. They both loved dancing, so their Friday nights were often spent together at the local swing dances.

Ernie's youth was centred around the local YMCA. Since most of the men were overseas fighting, Ernie was called upon to teach the activity classes at the centre. He also spent many evenings in the basement, working at the towel counter. For three summers, he headed up to the YMCA Boy's Camp to be a counsellor, leading youngsters in all manner of activities from rowing to archery. Through a connection at the camp, he was hired at the Bank of Toronto in 1946.

Being a bank teller was a tricky job. If the till turned up short, the teller had to pay the difference from his own pocket. Once, someone turned in a very ragged $100 bill. Ernie put it in the till, but at the end of the day couldn't find it anywhere. He had to pay the $100 himself—a significant loss since Christmas bonuses at the time were only $75.

When he was 21, Ernie proposed to Donna, the young woman he had met so many years earlier on the bus. They decided to marry—but there was a hitch. In those days, tellers making less than $1500 a year, like Ernie,were not permitted to marry. When he requested special permission, the head office simply gave him a raise to $1500.

Frequent moves were part and parcel of the banking profession at that time. In the beginning, the family would move to a new town every year or two as Ernie was transferred to new branches and different positions. Each new town brought new opportunities.

When they lived in Burford, their landlord drove school buses, and he asked Ernie to get his bus licence so he could be a substitute driver. The car Ernie was driving at the time was a 1937 Pontiac, which had passed through two previous owners. Needless to say, it was getting a little worse for the wear by the mid-1950s. When Ernie went to get his permit, the driver examiner took one look at the car and asked incredulously, "Does that even start?"

Ernie assured him that it did, and they set off on the test. At the first corner, the tester told him, "Turn left." He kept repeating that command at each stop sign until they were back at the permit office. They had simply driven around the block.

"If you can drive this damned thing, you can drive a bus!" The tester exclaimed, and gave him a pass.

Despite the driver's scepticism, that trusty car took Ernie

and his young family to the family cottage in White Lake many times. Before their third child was born, he and Donna put milk crates on the floor of the back seat and placed a crib mattress on top, making a comfortable bed for their son and daughter to sleep on during the long drives. They would spent weeks there every summer.

The family bounced across Ontario, from Mount Forest to Burlington. They spent several years in London, where Ernie took on extra work at the Western Fair racetrack. He first worked behind the counter and then moved upstairs to help calculate the value of the winning ticket. They were always under close supervision by the Mounties. In his spare time, he also built two sailboats in his garage and was a member of the Fanshawe Sailing Club.

While in London, Ernie fulfilled his lifelong goal of attending university, taking computer science and banking classes at the University of Western Ontario. At that time, there were no personal computers. Students used the mainframe computer at the university, which required punched cards to input programs and data. Ernie would return from a long day of work to an evening of homework, headphones on to block out the noise of his three youngsters. Although he was transferred to a new position in the Regional and Head Office in Toronto before he could finish his bachelor's degree, computers have remained an interest of his ever since.

Upon their retirement in 1989, Ernie and Donna moved to the cottage for several years where he enjoyed his hobby of sailing in the summer months. The winters were long and snowy, burying the laneway under deep drifts and allowing lots of time for Ernie to pursue his interest in wood carving.

In 2001, he suffered a stroke. They sold the cottage and moved to a new home in Lakefield. Now, after so many moves, they have at last settled in one more small town—Stratford—where they are close to their daughter.

Downtown Stratford in a Limousine

Shirley Davis

Shirley took a deep breath as she stepped on to the special train coach. It wasn't every day that she reported for work on a boxcar—but then, it wasn't every day that she worked for the Governor General of Canada either. The year was 1955, and the esteemed office was held by Vincent Massey at the time. He came to town on his personal train, staying to enjoy several productions at the new Stratford Festival Theatre.

A few weeks earlier Shirley had been taking dictation in the law office where she worked when she overheard her boss Wilfrid Gregory saying, "Shirley could do that." He was in conversation with Vic Polley, the business manager of the theatre.

"What is he getting me into?" she had wondered, but she soon found out. She was to be the Governor General's temporary secretary for the duration of his stay in Stratford.

One of Shirley Davis's earliest memories is looking out of the second-storey window of the Stratford train station, watching King George VI and his wife Queen Elizabeth of England waving from the back of their railway car below. Around them, throngs of people were gathered, cheering and waving Union Jacks. Nearly the whole town had come out to catch a glimpse of the royals on their brief stopover in Stratford, and Shirley had the best view of anyone. Her father, a CNR employee, worked in an office on the second floor, so he had brought her up to see. She pressed her face up against the glass, straining to take in the thin, handsome king and the elegantly-dressed queen.

Shirley grew up in a house on Ontario Street. She attended Stratford Collegiate Vocational Institute and worked part-time throughout high school at the Stratford General Hospital, and later as a file clerk in the train station. Every Saturday morning, she co-hosted a local radio show called 'Teen Town' with Lloyd Robertson, who went on to become a widely-recognized television broadcaster. After high school, Shirley took a year of Special Commercial to learn shorthand and then began a long career as a legal secretary.

For many years, Shirley worked for Wilfrid Gregory, a prominent Stratford lawyer who was instrumental in helping the Stratford Festival gain traction in its early years. Thanks to this connection, Shirley was involved with the theatre from the very start. When the Governor General Vincent Massey stopped in town, Shirley was enlisted to act as his secretary during his week-long stay. Massey was an ardent supporter of the arts, and his attendance at the Festival brought credibility and acclaim to the newly-minted theatre. Before the days of convenient air travel, the train was the fastest way to cross the country, so Massey had his own personal rail cars outfitted with offices and living quarters which simply needed to be attached to an engine. They could be taken wherever he needed to travel.

Each morning during his stay, Shirley set off for the train station. She got to know Massey's staff quite well, working alongside them and taking her lunches with them on the train. Both she and one of the aides were getting married in the summer, so they became friends through their discussions of their upcoming nuptials. While they were in Stratford, Massey's chief aide came down with a bad cold, so Shirley arranged an appointment for him with her own family doctor. They all rode together in a limousine to the doctor's office downtown.

Her work mainly consisted of typing out speeches that Massey would be making in the coming months, triple spaced. One of the speeches she typed was for the Boy Scouts' World Jamboree in Niagara Falls. Shirley had the thrill of watching him deliver that same speech on television later that summer. When the Governor General's cars pulled out of the Stratford station bound for their next destination, Massey gave Shirley a silver compact as a token of appreciation. His main secretary also sent her a congratulatory card when she was married later that year.

For the first few years after the Festival opened, Stratford was ill-prepared to handle the theatre guests arriving in town. There weren't many hotels, so the theatre kept a list of people who were willing to rent out rooms in their homes to visitors. They would call individually to organize the rooms for out-of-town patrons. Shirley's parents lived near the festival grounds, so they frequently boarded theatre-goers in their extra bedrooms. As it grew, the theatre began to attract many famous guests, including Lady Eaton, the wife of Eaton's Department Store owner Sir John Eaton. She stayed in a home across the street, but her chauffeur boarded at Shirley's parents' house. One evening when he wasn't working, the chauffeur took Shirley's whole family for a ride in the limo. It was a fun experience to glide up and down the familiar streets of their town in that majestic car.

Over the years, Shirley's support of the Stratford Festival has not waned. In 1984, she began volunteering as a Friend of the Festival in addition to the various other organizations to which she gives her time. Ever since, she has volunteered each season in various roles within the theatre. Currently, she can be found lending a hand in the costume warehouse.

Opportunity at the End of the Road
Cliff Taylor

Cliff watched the truck disappear into the dust of the highway, leaving him alone in the interior of northern British Columbia. Only that morning, he'd been at home in Chilliwack, waking up to milk the cows as he did every day. The quiet southern town was too small to contain his youthful ambition, so he left a note on the kitchen table for his parents. "I don't know where I'm going, but I'm going," it read. With that, he walked out to the highway and stuck out his thumb.

He'd been picked up by a couple of fellows in a truck heading north. When they reached a fork in the road, the driver asked him which way he was headed.

"Well, which way are you going?" Cliff responded. They told him they were going to the left, up to Prince George. "That's good enough for me," Cliff said.

They drove all day, nearly 700 km through dense forest and craggy mountains. Cliff got off outside Prince George and caught another ride north. Night was closing in by the time he was dropped off outside of Smithers. There on the side of the road, Cliff unrolled his sleeping bag, zipped himself in, and fell asleep.

He awoke in the darkness, suddenly aware that he was not alone. There was a snuffling sound as something nudged his sleeping bag. Looking down, he could make out the form of a hulking black bear, nosing around near his feet. Filling his lungs with air, he hollered as loudly as he could. The bear jumped back and lumbered off into the woods, leaving Cliff alone again with his heart beating loudly against his ribs.

Cliff Taylor was born in Toronto in 1918, but his family left the city far behind when he was only a baby, moving to a homestead in northern Saskatchewan. For $10, they purchased 160 acres of land and were charged with the task of turning the remote Prairie wilderness into a working farm. Most of his neighbourhood playmates were First Nations. He was eighteen when he first saw electricity.

The family was fortunate to escape the terrible drought and dust storms that plagued southern Saskatchewan and much of the prairies. Though there was never any excess, they always had three square meals a day throughout the Depression. Cliff's mother raised turkeys to sell in the fall for a little spending money, which she would use to buy fabric. As he grew older, Cliff grew restless. There was no opportunity there for young people, and he couldn't see a future spent on the farm. At eighteen, he and his brother headed south.

Their car took them all the way to Calgary before it broke down. From there, they joined the the hundreds of other young men riding the railroads in search of work. They climbed into an empty boxcar and rode it through the Rockies to British Columbia. They were never alone—at times, there could be up to sixteen men in a single car. Each had a destination in mind, somewhere that they'd heard might have work. Every time, they would arrive at their stop to find that it wasn't true: that place was no different from the last.

Sometimes, there wouldn't be any open boxcars, so Cliff would climb up to the walkway across the top of the car and hang on. It got cold with the wind rushing by, but sleeping outside was nothing out of the ordinary. The train engineers never questioned them or threw them off; they seemed to understand that most riders were honest men simply looking for a way to make a living.

The Okanagan apple-picking season was a godsend to riders. With 800 acres of orchards, fruit growers could hire as many men as were willing to toil under the hot sun for long hours. Cliff found work at a ranch in the Okanagan, picking apples and working in the hay field. The farm kept 2000 head of cattle, and when it came time to cut the hay, they needed 50 men for the job. Cliff stayed with family friends from Saskatchewan who worked permanently at the ranch. In the evenings, there wasn't much to do, so he often accompanied them to visit other families in the area. As the older people visited, Cliff got to know one of the rancher's daughters. Their courtship was cut short by the end of the apple season. With the colder weather encroaching, Cliff and his brother returned to the rails.

After some wandering, they finally found a man looking for someone to cut firewood. They spent the whole winter in the bush chopping down trees. The man couldn't pay them a penny, but he did offer a warm bed and food to fuel them through the day. Meanwhile, Cliff kept up a correspondence with the rancher's daughter, sending letters whenever he could.

Wishing to be closer to their sons, Cliff's parents bought a farm in Chilliwack, the province's dairy region. Cliff met them in Calgary to drive them through the mountains. His father had never driven before, and Cliff's mother was not willing to venture down the winding mountain roads with her husband behind the wheel. Cliff easily found work milking cows in Chilliwack, but he was again frustrated by the lack of opportunity there for him. For the second time, he set off from his parent's farm with an unknown path before him.

He hitchiked to Smithers, British Columbia, which was literally where the road ended. There was no work there either, so Cliff hopped onto a freight train bound for Prince Rupert, a port city on the North Coast. The train pulled in at 10 p.m., and he went directly to the town restaurant. There, his perseverance was finally rewarded. He sat down at the bar and asked the man next to him if there was any work to be found.

"You can work for me in the morning, if you want," the man said. He was a painter. Cliff had no experience with painting, so he politely declined. "Well, there's a government ship down at the harbour, and the captain is looking for men."

The very next morning, Cliff was waiting at the gangplank when the captain arrived. He was hired on the spot and began work that same day. The ship was responsible for looking after the buoys and lighthouses along the West Coast from Ketchikan, Alaska, all the way down to Vancouver Island. It was the kind of job he had dreamed about all those long nights spent in boxcars: secure, permanent, and well-paying. He wrote to the rancher's daughter in the Okanagan with marriage on his mind. After so many years of searching, he had finally found work.

The Day the Americans Came
Noel deWever

A young boy marched resolutely through the garden. Rows of well-trimmed bushes spotted with flowers flanked the path on either side. The air was filled with the drone of airplanes overhead, a sound which had grown familiar in recent months as the fighting intensified in the skies above the Netherlands. In the deep, dank basement of the large brick house behind him, his family and a few of his neighbours were crowded, protected against the threat of bombing. The young boy, however, had an independent spirit and was tired of cowering in the basement when he'd rather be outside.

All of a sudden, the ground around him erupted with bullets. They sent up puffs of dust as they hit the dirt, slicing through the air with a sharp noise. Immediately, the boy began running, through the garden, up the steps, and into the house. He paused at the door to look up at the sky—his far-away assailant was nowhere to be seen. It must have been an American plane shooting at him, thinking he was a German. Turning back to the house, he hurried inside to the safety of the basement.

Many of Noel deWever's early memories of growing up in the Netherlands are shadowed by the German occupation of his country during the Second World War. He was raised by his grandparents in a small hamlet in Limberg, the southernmost province of Holland. It was a sleepy place nestled among the hills, composed of only twenty other families.

The family in the courtyard of their home.

The deWevers were fortunate to live in the rural southern countryside, where fresh fruits and vegetables remained plentiful throughout the war. Only imported foods like coffee and tea were unavailable, but this didn't bother young Noel. It was the North which suffered from food shortages, which southerners could do nothing to alleviate because rail lines between the two areas were cut off.

The German influence made itself known in Noel's village in subtle ways at first. The movie theatres were overtaken by Nazi propaganda, so much that Noel's grandmother forbade him from going to the movies for the duration of the war. The family asserted their subversion in small ways—after radios were outlawed, the family hid their antenna, listening to the radio in secret in the cellar. The first serious run-in with the German authorities involved Noel's grandmother's profession. She worked for Social Services, removing children from abusive or inadequate homes and settling them in foster care or insitutions. The outbreak of the war gave unfit parents another tool in their arsenal to fight social services. When they were taken to court by Noel's grandmother, they complained to German officials that they were being prosecuted unfairly because of their loyalty to Germany. Noel recalls the day that German officials knocked on the front door asking to speak to his grandmother. He was very afraid that she would be taken away. Fortunately, she had proof of the family's mistreatment of their children, so she was able to show officials that her actions were justified. They realized they had to cooperate with her, as her job was very necessary. Still, the family had to be on the look-out for others in their community who would use the German occupation to their advantage. The deWevers' next door neighbour was known in the village as a traitor. They were careful of what they said and did, for fear of being reported to German authorities as disloyal.

Noel, after the war in 1950.

Each morning, Noel and his grandmother would drive into the city—Noel on his way to high school, his grandmother on the way to work. This commute became impossible after the Germans arrived to take the car away. The deWevers thwarted them by removing some of the parts so the car didn't work, but after that they had no choice but to take the bus. The bus was powered by shovelling coal into the back, which caused a terrible stench as it burned. As the war drew on, the city was shaken by bombings more and more frequently, so Noel stayed at home. Eventually even their little village became a target, sending the deWevers into their windowless basement. There was no need for sirens, because the planes were loud enough to be heard from miles away.

The backyard garden.

At last the Americans arrived to liberate his village, but it wasn't an easy task. Many homes and barns were destroyed by the intense fighting between Germans and Americans, while the villagers didn't dare venture from the safety of their homes. Noel's home was spared thanks to the particular landscaping of its backyard garden. There were four wide stone steps down the length of the yard. Seeing the steps, the approaching Americans decided it would be easier to go around than to try to haul their heavy equipment and tanks over them. The garden was left undisturbed.

When they finally succeeded in driving the Germans out, the whole town was alive with celebrations. People finally felt safe to leave their house and walk—even dance—freely through the streets. The American soldiers stayed on for nearly a year, boarding in the deWevers' house because it was the biggest in the village. Six officers stayed with them, eating at their dinner table and flirting with his sisters. "My grandmother put a stop to that," Noel chuckles. They ate a lot of food and made a lot of laundry. However, they had brought the end of the war to Noel's village, so they were treated with the utmost hospitality and gratitude.

The Lucky Pony
Bill and Lorna Switzer

Another warm summer's day in Stratford had nearly come to a close. The crack of the bat from the nearby ball field could be heard in the distance amidst the buzz of cicadas, and the garden glowed in the warm light of the sunset. Bill and his eldest son were just packing up their work on the house's new addition when Bill noticed his daughter approaching—accompanied by a man leading a pony on a rope. The look on her face was one that every parent recognizes. It said, 'Can we keep it?'

Lorna and Bill Switzer have lived for most of their lives in a house on Simcoe Street. When they moved in, the house was on the edge of town, but in the years since, they have seen subdivisions rise around them, old schools torn down and new ones built, and new developments that have extended the city on all sides. In 1975, however, their home was still surrounded by open space, reminiscent of the farms on which both Bill and Lorna were raised. In small-town Stratford, there were plenty of activities to keep their four small children busy, along with many of the neighbourhood kids. Nearby, the drive-in theatre played new releases, and the mini-golf course offered an afternoon diversion. But most of the fun could be found in their own backyard. The woods of the municipal golf course backed onto the Switzers' lot, and their children spent hours among the trees, where tree forts housed secret societies and make-believe games. Between the Switzers' four children and the many neighbourhood kids,

129

the house was always busy. Their home really became the neighbourhood favourite after the Switzers' daughter won the pony raffle.

The pony raffle was an annual event at the family baseball game, which speaks to the rural nature of Stratford at that time. For girls who had grown up watching *International Velvet* and *Black Beauty*, it was a coveted prize. That year, Bill and his sons were busy digging the foundation for their new addition, so their daughter went to the baseball game at the nearby diamond without them. When the moment of the raffle arrived, the winning ticket belonged to Bill and Lorna's daughter!

Understanding that many city folk could not keep a pony, the owner had planned to take it back if the raffle winner turned out to be a town dweller. However, he had gone home before the draw, leaving the organizers with a pony on their hands, and no idea what to do with it. One of them accompanied the Switzers' daughter home to speak with her parents to see if it would be all right for her to keep it.

It was the organizers' lucky day as well—the Switzers did not balk when they saw the pony trotting into their yard. They already kept a cow which they pastured in the summer, and a few pigs and chickens, so the addition of a pony to their backyard menagerie was welcomed. Lorna admits there was "some scurrying around" that night to figure out just what to do with this unexpected equine who came with nothing but the bridle she was wearing. In the end, they tied her to a tree in the backyard for the night. The next day, their work on the addition was temporarily halted as they turned their attention to building a stable for the horse. They decided to name her 'Lucky,' a nod to her fortuitous path to their possession.

Lucky quickly became a favourite in the neighbourhood. They built a little cart to hitch her up to, and the kids had hours of fun careening up and down the road. One of the neighbourhood girls took a special liking to the pony, and she would come over to comb and ride Lucky even when the Switzers weren't home. That little pony provided many hours of fun, not just for their family but for the whole neighbourhood.

And as for the pony raffle? In later years, they changed the prize to a bicycle, reflecting the growth of Stratford from small rural town to burgeoning city.

The Switzer's farm in the city.

Around the World. . . On a Container Ship

Harold May

On the grass between the two men, the latest in lawn mowing technology sat gleaming in the sunshine. It was an electric lawn-mower, the first of its kind to be sold in Canada. Its red surface was shiny and enticing, promising to make lawn-mowing an adventure rather than a weekly drudgery. Harold had been travelling across the province to local hardware stores promoting the new product.

"Just tell your customers this," Harold began. "It's a lot like a vacuum. Buy one of these, and your wife will be mowing the lawn."

Whether is was Harold's salesmanship or simply the convenience of the product itself, electric lawn mowers took off. It wasn't long before they were found in the garages and sheds of many homes across the country.

Harold May was the third generation in his family to own a business on the main street of St. Marys. Growing up, he worked alongside his father and grandfather in the dry goods store that they owned. His father had some health problems which the doctor thought would be remedied by outdoor work, so the family moved to Grimsby Beach to operate a peach farm and 32 acres of grapes. Harold helped out, driving the tractor from nine years of age up. However, those were Depression days, and the prices were terrible. Their peaches would sell for 20 cents a basket, only to be marked up and sold at the market in Montreal for $2. Harold's father often commented, "I never made any money on the farm, but I raised my family, so that's all right."

With the beginning of the war, the family returned to St. Marys. Harold's father took a job at a Chevrolet dealership, but that soon fizzled out as cars ceased to be manufactured. Only those whose professions demanded it were allowed to buy new cars. Harold's dad had a 1936 Ford whose tires were becoming threadbare so he traded cars with his cousin, a truant officer in the country who drove a 1929 Chevrolet. His cousin was able to outfit the Ford with new tires because he depended on his car for work. It seemed like a poor trade, but with no way of buying tires himself, it was the only way Harold's father could continue driving.

Harold's father, grandfather, and brother all worked for Maxwell's, a former lawnmower manufacturer that had been converted to make grenades for the war. Harold did his bit in wartime production as well, taking a part-time job at Richardson Foundry. Every day after school, he'd bike to the factory and spend the evening working on the lathe, which he'd learned to operate in shop class. He made the plug which went into the top of bombs, where the detonator would be placed once the bomb was safely shipped overseas and loaded with explosives. It was a very sombre task for a thirteen-year-old, but one that needed to be done.

When the war ended, it was a challenge to find work because so many veterans were returning from service. Harold set off on his motorcycle looking for a job, ending up at the hardware store in Woodstock. It was a simple clerking job, but he worked his way up through the ranks. He also met his wife Doris at a YWCA singles dance, and they settled in Woodstock.

Eventually, Harold became a commercial traveller. In this position, he travelled across Ontario to every mom-and-pop hardware store in each small town, selling small appliances and hardware supplies. In the prosperous post-war years, consumer goods were flying off the shelves as new homes went up across the country. With the Depression and war years behind them, people were eager to have the latest conveniences and luxuries in their homes. The forties and fifties were a great time to be in the hardware business, and Harold was right at the forefront. Along with the first electric lawnmower, he also sold the first paint rollers in Ontario. The salesman who sold the most electric Christmas light displays across Canada was Harold May. In appreciation, he was awarded a trip to Bermuda.

As a commercial traveller, Harold would leave on Monday morning and return Friday evening, covering a territory which spanned from Windsor to Georgian Bay, and as far north as Timmins. He enjoyed life on the road, but after a while it began to have its drawbacks. On weekend strolls around the neighbourhood, Doris would greet everyone she met, but Harold didn't know any of them. It was draining to be away from his family so much, so Harold left commercial travelling and began a 21 year career with Mutual Life. The hardware business was already starting to change: Canadian Tire and Home Hardware were growing into what would become vast hardware empires. The big box stores that now dominate the industry were just beginning to encroach. Today, not one of Harold's former customers is still in business.

In the 1970s, Harold returned to St. Marys with Doris and their two children. They purchased a furniture store on the main street which his wife ran, while he continued to sell life insurance. Every four years, Harold and Doris would travel to the Mutual Life national conference, which was always held in a different Canadian city. When he left Mutual Life, Harold drove the delivery truck for his wife, bringing new furniture to living rooms across the county. Throughout his life, he was an active member of the Lions Club, serving with them for over fifty years including three terms as president.

After his retirement, Harold traded business trips for pleasure trips. For years, he had joked that he would take Doris around the world on their fiftieth anniversary. The opportunity to make good on his light-hearted promise arose through an unconventional travel arrangement. He heard of a travel agency which specialized in container ship cruises. With more advanced computers, container ships didn't need to carry as many crewmen, so they rented out the extra cabins to tourists. Intrigued, he called the number and booked a cruise the next day.

Harold and Doris preparing to embark.

His wife could hardly believe it when he told her about the trip. They soon found themselves heading around the world on a huge container ship. For $100 a day, they stayed in the luxurious owner's suite and ate at the captain's table, stopping at various exotic destinations along the way.

While docked in Jakarta, Indonesia, the boat was struck

Doris, in front of the ship docked in Brisbane.

by pirates. Much more inconspicuous than the peg-legged buccaneers of legend, this pirate simply boarded the boat in disguise as the port officer's assistant, found a master key, and stole valuables from the cabins while most of the passengers were on land touring the city. Harold lost a large sum of money but was able to recover it eventually through insurance. After this rattling experience, they spent ten days in Singapore while the boat was being painted. They had a chance to explore the city in depth and become familiar with some of the main landmarks. The ninety day excursion took them to parts of the world they had never imagined they would see.

After a career spent in the driver's seat, Harold was content to sit back and enjoy the journey.

A Good Old-Fashioned Yarn
Laurene Zehr

In the one-room schoolhouse, a small group of girls sat in a cluster near the stove. The hoot of the boys, outside at recess, could be heard over the clicking of needles as the girls added row upon row to their knitting patches. Laurene looked at the needles in her hand with deep concentration. She wound the yarn around, slipped the needle out, and looped it onto the other needle. Beside her, the teacher nodded, demonstrating on her own needles. At the end of the lunch hour, she cast off her stitches carefully and dropped the completed strip into the basket. They had nearly finished enough to sew them into an afghan that would soon be sent overseas to a soldier.

Laurene Zehr's family farm is located south of Shakespeare on Pork Road. According to local lore, the road's distinctive name originates from an incident long before Laurene's time when several families living along that road had pork stolen from their smokehouses. Laurene's early life revolved around the farm. The bread delivery man came in their lane twice a week peddling his loaves for 9 cents apiece. The butcher also came weekly in the summer months. When he arrived, the kids would abandon whatever they had been doing to gather around his car, hoping for a free wiener to snack on. During the wartime, the Victory Bonds man also visited door-to-door, raising money for the war effort.

Laurene's father bought a car when she was a young child, and at first, she wasn't sure what to make of the loud, strange contraption. When her father pulled into the driveway for the first time and entreated her to take a ride, she ran back into the house and refused to come out. Electricity was a later development, illuminating Laurene's home in 1949. Until then, rooms were lit with coal oil lamps. Every Saturday morning, it was Laurene's job to refill all the lamps and clean their chimneys. At that time, it was common to plug the spout of the oil can with a gumdrop if the cap was missing. Occasionally, children would grow desperate for a taste of sugar and eat the candy off of the can. Although it was distinctively coal-oil-flavoured, they never got a sore throat when they ate those. It was a common remedy to swallow a few drops of coal oil mixed with sugar to cure a scratchy throat.

The family had a battery-operated radio which was turned on every Saturday night when Laurene's brother and father listened to the hockey game. The signal would fade as the battery ran down, so Laurene and her sisters had to tiptoe around the house so the men could hear the commentary. The schoolhouse they attended didn't have electricity either, and on a grey day it was difficult to see the blackboard.

Laurene (second row to the back, far left) and her classmates.

After grade eight, the inspector recommended that Laurene continue to high school, but there was no money to pay for boarding in Stratford. Instead, she moved into Tavistock at age fifteen and began work at the woollen mill. She started there shortly before the war ended, and they were still busy knitting socks for soldiers. It wasn't long before Laurene knew everybody in the small town of Tavistock. At that time, you could walk into any shop and the storekeeper would greet you by name, even dropping an extra little bag of candy into your shopping bag if he knew you had kids at home. There wasn't a lot to do during the evenings besides visiting. Laurene recalls attending a hockey game at a local arena once—but it took her so long to warm up afterwards that she vowed never to go again.

Laurene (right) and her sister.

Each morning, the women heading to the woollen mills would pass the men heading to Zimmerman's box factory, Tavistock's other main employer. The wool arrived at the mill freshly sheared in a raw state. First, it was carded and spun onto big cones, a heavy job which was done by men. Next, the spools were sent to the knitting machines, where

Laurene worked alongside twenty other women. With cylindrical machines, they knitted the thick wool into sturdy grey work socks with a white toe, heel, and cuff. Sometimes, they would add a red stripe around the top, which was a great annoyance because it meant switching yarns on the machine. After the toes were sewn shut, the socks were washed and put onto wooden forms which helped them keep their shape. Finally, they would be paired, packaged, and shipped across Canada.

Laurene enjoyed her days among the noisy knitting machines. It was fast-paced and fun to be with so many other women. They worked from 7 a.m. until 6 p.m. with an hour for lunch but no coffee breaks. Since they were paid by piecework, any time the machine was idle meant money was being lost. Once she got the hang of it, Laurene could turn out eight dozen socks a day—the record in the factory was nine dozen. The knitters had to be exact in their work, because each sock would be checked for dropped stitches. If a needle broke and a stitch was lost, the sock had to be mended and placed in the seconds pile. Knitters who produced too many seconds would be reprimanded.

Every summer, the woollen mills closed down for two weeks, giving all the workers a holiday. Their vacation always began with the annual band tattoo in the Tavistock Park, where the community would gather on the bleachers to watch local bands perform. Laurene always spent her two week holiday on the farm, where there was never a shortage of work to be done during the summer months, from raspberry-picking to fieldwork.

After seven-and-a-half years at the woollen mill, Laurene left the job to get married to a man she had met at a Young People's Meeting in Tavistock. Their wedding reception was held at her home farm, where her mother served crocks of potato salad, jelly salad, cold meat, and fresh rolls, finishing the meal off with banana cupcakes. Laurene and her new

Laurene and her husband on their wedding day.

husband moved to their own farm, where they raised five children. In the evenings after the day's work was finished, Laurene still found time for knitting—on needles, this time, not the machine.

New Home, Old Memories
Mariechen Evers

"Mom, come quick!" Mariechen followed her son to the railing of the boat which had been their home for the past week. They had been anchored outside the harbour at Quebec City all night. Now, just as the sun was beginning to burn off the morning mist over the water, they were finally preparing to dock. Her son and two nephews jostled around her in their efforts to see over the railing.

"Look! I see Daddy!" her son squealed, bouncing as his little finger pointed into the distance. Mariechen squinted across the water. High on the bluffs, she could see the imposing Chateau Laurier looming over the city. The harbour was still merely a blur in the distance. They were too far away to see her husband, but she knew he would be there, waiting to meet them. She smiled down at her son and ruffled his hair. Secretly, she was just as excited as he was.

Mariechen Evers was born in 1927 on an estate in Schleswig-Holstein, the northernmost province of Germany. Her father's job was to care for the estate's 42 horses, and her mother milked the cows along with the other village women. In all the time they worked there, they had never met the owner, a very wealthy man who had four such estates across the province.

Along with most of the other workers and their families, Mariechen lived in a little village on the estate itself. Each

142

Mariechen is seated on the chair, beside her sister.

family had its own plot of land on which to keep a cow and a few pigs, as well as a portion of the field in which to grow their own potatoes. Potatoes were the staple of Mariechen's dinner table; they never had a meal without them. Another staple was bread—thick rye bread that her mother baked in a big batch each week. She made the dough in the afternoon and left it to rise overnight. Then, she built a fire inside the stone oven. Once it had burned down, she emptied out the coals and slid in the loaves of bread. The loaves were baked by the heat that the stones still held. Once the bread was done, the oven was cooled to the right temperature to bake cakes. Each week she would make eight to ten loaves, enough to fill the hungry bellies of her large family.

This changed when the war came. There was no flour to buy, so families were given coupons for store-bought bread to replace their hearty homemade loaves. They had to cover their windows with black material at night so not a single shred of light could be seen by airplanes overhead. Beyond these small changes the family did not notice the war much.

Mariechen (far right) with her siblings.

The northern area where they lived was purely agricultural, so it was spared the bombing to which the industrial southern cities were subjected. Many times they were completely unaware of the war events. Mariechen remembers her father turning on the radio, and her mother saying to him, "Why do you listen to that? It's all lies."

The war's end was overshadowed by personal tragedy for Mariechen's family, as her mother was quite ill at the time. She was pregnant with her tenth child, and there were many complications. After VE Day, British soldiers were in the area waiting to be sent home, and the family called for an army doctor to tend to the birth. Sadly, it was to no avail. The baby did not survive.

Life on the estate changed after the war. The owner had been a Nazi party official, so the property was confiscated and given to new owners from eastern Germany. One day, a new blacksmith arrived in the village. After a few months, Mariechen's father remarked that suddenly she seemed to have an awful lot of business at the blacksmith shop. All those visits blossomed into a romance, and the two were married soon after.

The blacksmith job was temporary, and taxes were high in Germany, so Mariechen's husband soon cast his eyes farther afield. His brother was already in Canada, and after

many fruitless applications, Mariechen's husband was finally accepted to join him. He left first, and Mariechen joined him later with her eight-year-old son, her sister-in-law, and two nephews. The boat ride over was rather rocky—at dinner, they would have to put boards on the ends of the tables so the dishes and cutlery didn't slide off. There was a swimming pool and games room to keep the children occupied, so they got along well on the journey. She was glad to reunite with her husband and proceed to their new home in Montreal, which he had already furnished and set up.

In Canada, old traditions mixed with new. As a child in Germany, Mariechen and her siblings used to polish their shoes and leave them on the windowsill on December the sixth. During the night, Santa would come to fill the shoe with chocolates, cookies, or other little surprises. Back on the estate, one person would be sent to a Christmas tree farm to bring back a truck full of trees. Then they would draw names for each tree, randomly assigning one tree to each family. Sometimes they would trade amongst themselves, but they never got to choose. The tree would not be decorated until Christmas Eve and was kept a surprise from the children until the morning.

One early December day in Montreal, Mariechen's daughter asked why they had no tree. All of her friends already had their trees up, and she was concerned that Santa wouldn't come if she didn't have one. They decided there was no harm in modifying their traditions. They all went together one evening to a tree lot nearby to choose one. Her daughter helped to carry it home, singing Christmas carols all the way.

A new holiday that they had to adjust to was Halloween. The first year she was in Canada, Mariechen was caught off guard by the groups of small ghosts and goblins ringing her doorbell. They had never heard of Halloween back home and were not prepared. She had to run down to the corner store to pick up some candy for the trick-or-treaters.

Over the years, she returned to Germany more times than she can count, bringing her children to meet their grandparents and travelling around Europe. Her daughter was a horse lover like Mariechen's father, so she was very excited to visit the horses on the estate—though by then, tractors had replaced all but two of them. Mariechen has travelled across Canada to both coasts, living in Montreal and Edmonton, and moving only recently to Stratford. She holds a special fondness for the Germany of her childhood while cultivating a deep love for her adopted country as well.

Life on the Carnival Circuit
Ruth Spooner

The sun was just starting to warm the carnival grounds, hinting at another hot summer's day to come. At the entrance, the flags stirred in a light wind. Cheerful music from the Ferris wheel wafted across the air which also carried the ever-present scent of candy floss and popcorn, a sweet and salty mixture. In the entrance booth, rolls of red tickets sat curled and ready for the crowds.

It was quiet at Ruth's trailer, but not for long. The vivid orange gold fish drifted in their bowls of colourful water. They flicked their tails, unaware that soon they would become a treasured prize for some lucky child. The rows of glass bowls enticed onlookers to take a shot. Ruth looked up at the first sounds of children's voices, echoing with excitement as they entered the grounds. She smiled. Another day at the carnival was beginning.

Ruth Spooner's life as a carny began when she married her husband, who already had several years of experience in the business. They decided to venture together into children's games, first with the well-known Conklin shows, then with a variety of smaller carnivals. They bought a trailer and set up the classic Goldfish Game, in which players try to sink their ping pong ball into the glass bowl with the fish in it. If you've ever seen children wandering the fairgrounds with a big smile and a fish swimming inside a plastic bag, chances are good that they've just won the Goldfish Game.

Every spring, the excitement would build as Ruth and her husband prepared to go out on the road for another season. They invested a lot of time during the winter months sprucing up the trailer with new coats of paint and new equipment. There were lots of errands at home to prepare for six months on the road. Finally, when the days started to grow longer and summer beckoned, they would pack up their house trailer, hitch on the games trailer, and drive off. The carnival circuit took them to every corner of Ontario, from small towns to big cities.

Life on the road was busy, draining—and fun. After driving to their destination, Ruth and her husband parked their trailer at the fairgrounds. A whole day would be spent setting up and preparing. At each stop, they had to buy new fish which they stored in an aerated barrel. They would fill and aerate each glass bowl, distribute the fish, and arrange the bowls in the trailer.

From the time the gates opened in the morning until the last sleepy child went home at night, Ruth was on her feet, taking money, making change, distributing ping pong balls, and chasing after the ones that flew haphazardly from children's hands. For one dollar, carnival-goers would get a sand pail full of ping pong balls, each with the potential to win a fish. Children would flock to the game, but sometimes the adults were just as eager. Ruth could only shake her head at the parents who would haggle with their children for a chance to throw the balls. At the end of the day, each fish would have to be retrieved from its bowl to spend the night in the larger barrel. Then the water had to be changed and the trailer freshened up for the next day. After three or four days, they would pack it all away again and drive to the next location.

Over time, Ruth developed a kinship with the other carnival workers who travelled with them to each place. Everyone was willing to help each other, lending an extra hand when needed. It makes Ruth sad to hear the stereotypes people attach to carnies—that they're mean, rough, or even dishonest people. During her time in the carnival, she was touched by their kindness and friendliness.

Of course, it wasn't easy work—there were long hours on the road, the risk of rainstorms which could ruin a weekend, and the constant competition between games. Despite the challenges, there was joy in every day. It was impossible not to join in with the children's delighted laughter and their pure elation at winning something as small as a goldfish.

After her husband's death, Ruth left the carnival lifestyle behind her, moving on to new places. She still looks back fondly on her years with the goldfish, remembering the smiles on kids' faces, all the happy moments she witnessed, and the friends she made along the way. Though much time has passed since those days, she still considers herself to be a carny at heart.

The Lion's Jamboree
Marjorie Ballantyne

Marjorie climbed carefully up the stairs to her bedroom, treading lightly. She knew it was later than midnight, but she hadn't even noticed the time passing. Her mind was reeling from the evening's events.

Earlier that afternoon, she and her mother had been at the Lion's Jamboree, wandering from booth to booth and chatting with neighbours. It was a rainy day in June, and Marjorie had the bad luck of stepping straight into a puddle. She and her mother had been there for a little while when they passed a group of young men. One of them was a childhood acquaintance whom she hadn't seen for years.

"Oh, hi Bob," Marjorie said nonchalantly, continuing on her way. A few moments later, Bob was back at her side, inviting her to the dance at the Blue Room that evening. Wet feet and all, Marjorie went, spinning around the dance floor all evening with Bob. When he drove her home, they sat in the front seat talking for what felt like hours, even though Bob's friend was still in the backseat waiting to be driven home as well.

As Marjorie tiptoed past her parent's bedroom, her mother came to the door. "How did that go?"

"I think I'm going to marry that boy," Marjorie replied.

Exactly one year later, she did.

Marjorie Ballantyne's parents arrived in Canada on a ship that docked in Halifax shortly after the famous explosion which destroyed much of the city in 1917. Though they were from England, they decided to settle in Quebec, where Marjorie's father, a chemist, got a job at a paint factory. Marjorie and her sister were born there and spent their early years living in a second story apartment in Saint Lambert.

The apartment had a balcony which looked out onto the street, and one morning the girls were playing together there. Someone had left a couch up against the railing, and Marjorie's sister, then two years old, was able to climb up and lean over. She was delighted to discover that if she held her yo-yo over the railing, she could roll it along the sidewalk below. Again and again she did this, leaning further out each time until she suddenly toppled over, falling down onto the concrete sidewalk. Marjorie clearly recalls running after her parents' car as it sped away with her sister inside, calling, "Mommy! Mommy!" Her sister had a fractured skull, but fortunately she made a full recovery.

The spicy odour of mustard pervaded Marjorie's childhood. She seemed to catch a cold every two weeks throughout her school days, so her mother would mix up a paste of mustard powder and flour, put it between two moist cloths, and apply it to her chest. The plasters got very hot and helped to relieve congestion—though they were quite unpleasant for a six-year-old. Marjorie's mother would sit by her bed and help her with homework so she didn't fall behind in school.

Her parents had left all their relatives behind in England, so they encouraged Marjorie and her sister to consider their close friends 'uncle' and aunt.' One such uncle was Dan McArthur, son of the author Peter McArthur. Dan McArthur and her father began experimenting with copper engraving. Her father used his chemistry background to take care of the science behind it while Dan contributed his artistic flair. They made copper plates to print Christmas cards and some wall-hangings, all of which now reside in the Royal Ontario Museum.

When Marjorie was 15, the family moved to Stratford, where Marjorie's father got a job in the newly-formed rubber division of Griffith's Harness Factory. Marjorie remained in Stratford to attend the Normal School, becoming a teacher. She taught for a short while in Galt before getting married. On the morning of the wedding, the groom's car broke down en route to the church. He had to walk "full steam," but he arrived in time. His friends managed to get it working again in time for them to depart for their honeymoon in Ottawa.

Marjorie and her husband moved into an old farmhouse near Avonton, which they spent many years fixing up. Her husband took a night course in wiring so that he could outfit the house with hydro. Marj had spent the previous Easter with her husband's family, so she had learned some of the necessary farm skills from her mother-in-law. Working 300 acres and raising five children kept the couple very busy, but Marjorie's memories from that time are happy ones.

She loved to watch her husband play with the children; he would bounce them on his knee, play songs for them on the mouth organ, and spend time listening attentively to their stories. She grew accustomed to setting out extra plates for family and friends dropping in for a visit on their way home from the lake. In spite of her urban beginnings, Marjorie was a true country girl by the time they retired to Stratford after over 20 years on the farm.

Marjorie and her daughter feeding the swans.

The Mess Hall Strike

Joseph Hart

The cavernous mess hall was strangely silent that morning; there was no clinking of silverware or rattling of trays. The usual din of chatter was replaced by uneasy shuffling as the men sat stony-faced in front of empty tables. It was two months after the war's end at a compound outside of Hamburg, Germany.

The orderly arrived, his face turning red as he surveyed the scene. "I order you all to get breakfast and return to work, now."

Nobody moved. The men had been stuck in limbo long enough, waiting to hear when they'd be sent home while the food steadily grew less palatable. Now, they were down to tins of bully beef left over from the First World War. They had endured enough, and they were taking a stand.

Some time later, the sound of a motor was heard outside. Flanked by military police and personnel, the brigadier marched in, climbed onto a table and shouted at the men. "If you don't get back to your duty immediately, I will have every third man on the roster shot."

The hall, quiet for so long, erupted in "boo's," drowning out the rest of his words. Recognizing the volatility of the crowd, he left the hall quickly with the military police close behind. The men would not leave the hall that day until they had been promised an improvement in the food and a date for their return home.

154

Joseph Hart was born to a railroad family. His father and brother both worked for the CNR in Toronto, where he was raised. At the age of 17, he set off down the tracks to Stratford, beginning his five-year apprenticeship in the shops. He found himself in the hub of the railroad industry, boarding in a house on Nile Street, a stone's throw from the station. Apprentices trained under the regular mechanics, rotating between all of the different areas. At the time, the shops employed over 1200 men. Joseph started in the machine shop working with a drill press and then moved to the wrecking-shop, where locomotives were assembled, making 30 cents an hour. In his spare time, he spent many evenings at the local YMCA, which was located on the same property as the CNR shops. The shops supplied heat to the building because they had so much excess steam.

Shortly before he turned eighteen, Joseph went to London to enlist for the army. It was 1941, and he knew he'd be called up soon anyways. After his training in Kingston was complete, he boarded the *New Amsterdam*, a converted pleasure ship that had been outfitted with a gun on the back. Early one morning, an alarm went out calling everyone to their stations. Joseph scrambled out of his hammock, but the other man in his cabin just rolled over. "If the ship's sinking, there's nothing I can do about it now," he mumbled as he fell back to sleep. In the end, it was a false alarm, and they made the crossing safely. They landed in England around the same time as the D-Day invasion.

Despite only getting into their billets at midnight, the men had to be on the parade square at six a.m. for their first full day in England. There, the group was divided into two— one half was to be artillery and the other half infantry. Joseph found himself on the infantry side. They boarded another boat bound for Antwerp, Belgium, and from there, the men were posted to different regiments which had suffered heavy casualties and needed reinforcements.

With his regiment, Joseph travelled through most of Belgium and northern Holland, passing the long rows of windmills and cities ravaged by bombings. Then, they crossed the Rhine into Germany. They made the crossing in a big Buffalo water-and-land tank which was open at the top. The current was so strong that they drifted far downstream before finally making their landing. The situation only got worse when they found themselves in an ammunition dump. The area around them was littered with old machinery, ammunition, tanks, and other war materials that had been left behind in the German retreat. Since they were being shelled constantly, they knew the whole place could go up at any moment.

The order was given for the men to find themselves a slit trench. Joseph jumped into the nearest one he saw, landing right on top of a slippery, squealing pig! It had fallen in and become trapped in the hole. In the cramped 2 by 6 foot trench, Joseph had no choice but to sit on the pig throughout the shelling, hoping it wouldn't get "too rambunctious." Once the shelling quieted down, the men did some exploring around the site, stopping to take a look at some V1 flying bombs which had been dumped. Nicknamed 'buzz bombs,' they had been used extensively during the German bombing campaign against England.

Joseph's unit was in Hamburg when the war ended, and he volunteered to stay on for occupation duty. Their main job was to maintain order in the city; many civilians were starving, and the fighting in the streets increased with their desperation. Joseph's regiment stayed in a former German army compound outside the city. Desperation soon began to build within the Canadian troops as well, as the weeks passed with no word on when they would be sent home. Every day the quality of the food worsened, and the men became more restless.

The situation came to a head in the form of a strike,

which was organized by some men in Joseph's compound. Everyone but the guards gathered in the mess hall but refused to eat their breakfast. The authorities tried to call in another regiment to do their duties, but the other regiment shared the strikers' grievances, so they refused to get involved. The afternoon wore on with no movement, until finally their well-liked company colonel was able to negotiate. He assured strikers that their point had been made—and he was right. Three weeks later, Joseph was on a boat heading through the Baltic Sea. He spent another week in a camp in southern England before a ship arrived. Its intended passengers, a group of war brides, were pulled from the ship, and Joseph's regiment was allowed to embark.

The journey home was made more pleasant by an Air Force chap who had a special talent on the piano. He'd entertain the others after dinner in the dining hall, playing any song they requested in any style they could come up with. After his return, Joseph had two week's leave before he was back at the CNR shops, completing his apprenticeship. He became certified as a machinist and married the girl who lived next door to his boarding-house on Nile Street. Her family, too, was deeply entrenched in the rail business. Her father had been the stationmaster at Goderich, and both grandfathers had worked on the railway—one for CNR and the other for CPR.

Nineteen years after he began at the CNR shops, Joseph lost his job due to the major cutbacks which accompanied the move from steam to diesel engines. The face of the railway industry was changing, and its future in Stratford was uncertain, so Joseph moved on to other things. He became the custodian of the Stratford Police Station, working there for another 29 years before his retirement. He never lost his mechanical inclinations, however. His home today is filled with clocks, trains, and other collectibles, reflecting his fascination with "things that move."

The Adventures of Teaching
Alice Wilson

The young woman stood at the front of the classroom. Forty kindergarten students looked innocently back at her. They were scrubbed and polished for their first day of school, and their eager faces surveyed Alice with as much trepidation as she felt facing such a large class on her own. The postwar baby boom had flooded schools with students, and school boards could hardly keep up with the demand for new schools, new classrooms, and new teachers. This class was meant to have an assistant, but she hadn't yet been hired. So, for the time being, Alice was left alone to lead the forty youngsters in crafts, story-time, and songs, guiding them through their first day of school.

Alice Wilson grew up in Monkton, Ontario, the daughter of the town's general storekeeper. She spent much of her youth among the shelves, first helping out with small tasks like stocking, and later moving up to serving customers, measuring out coal oil, and wheeling in the large sacks of flour and sugar that would pass through the store each week. There was no cash register, so she became very adept at arithmetic, adding all the bills by hand. The store carried a little bit of everything—groceries, of course, as well as patent drugs, material and thread, shoes, boots, and overalls. There was an egg grading station in the basement to process the eggs which nearby farmers would bring to exchange for grocery staples. At that time, farmers and grocers relied on each other to stay afloat. During the sparse years of the Depression when everyone was merely scraping by, the grocer would allow families to buy goods on credit if they didn't have the money up-front. Later during the war, when rationing put a strain on the store's resources, the storekeepers relied on farmers to supply them with butter and other goods to keep the shelves full.

While the store was a fixture of her childhood, school was always Alice's passion, though she wouldn't have admitted it at the time. She and her brother were the first students to be bused into high school in Mitchell; prior to that, students had to board or find their own ride to the larger town. Upon completion of high school, Alice decided to follow her love of learning further. She enrolled in the Stratford Normal School, where she trained to become a teacher.

Alice (far right) on the steps of the Normal School.

Alice moved into a room in a little house on the edge of what is now the Festival Theatre grounds. In those days, the theatre hadn't yet been built, so there was only parkland between the red brick school building on the hill and the river below. The rigorous schedule of classes and practice teaching left the girls with little time to spare. During the day, they learned how to teach all of the main subjects: mathematics, social studies, science, primary reading, and phonics. Each evening, they would spend time preparing lesson plans for their weekly practice teaching, when they would be sent to local schools to experience life at the front of the classroom.

Besides the basics of teaching, the Normal school sought to groom their students to be pillars of the community. They emphasized the value of citizenship and encouraged students to teach Sunday School or lead Canadian Girls in Training groups on their own time. In 1946, after only one year of college, Alice and her classmates graduated and set off for classrooms across the province. Most of them were only nine-teen years old, teaching students who were sometimes only a few years younger than themselves. Nevertheless, they were full of enthusiasm and ambition, and Alice marvels at what they managed to accomplish.

Teaching students doing the school cheer.
Alice is second from the right.

After graduation, a former neighbour from Monkton told Alice that the school in Goderich was hiring a kindergarten assistant. Alice had always wanted to teach kindergarten, but it required an additional qualification of Primary School Specialist. She applied for the assistant position, and that September began her teaching career in Goderich, working with a kindly older teacher. The next summer, she completed the primary specialization courses, and before long she was at the front of her own class. For the rest of her career, Alice saw countless classes of kindergarteners walk through her doors, each with their own joys and challenges. She also taught music, which was always strong in Perth County schools. At the time, itinerant music teachers travelled to multiple schools in the district, visiting each school on a weekly basis to teach students to read notes and sing in parts. The school concerts and operettas were always a highlight of the year. Once, Alice directed an operetta performance of *Hansel and Gretel* which was reviewed by the London Free Press.

When busy school days gave way to summer holidays, Alice and her friends discovered a creative way to find adventure on a teacher's scanty budget. At the time, it was common practice for car dealerships to let people deliver new cars from Ontario to their owners on the West Coast. They had to pay for their own gas, but drivers had free use of the car for the allotted time, providing an inexpensive way to see the country! On their first trip, Alice and three others drove out to Vancouver in one of these cars. They took a leisurely path, stopping along the way in Banff and driving through the Rocky Mountains. It was breath-taking.

Each summer for the next three years, they drove out to the West, delivered the car, and spent the summer making their way down the West coast. During these travels, they saw the Grand Canyon, Old Faithful in Yellowstone National Park, Salt Lake City, and the beautiful landscapes of Wyoming and the Dakotas. Usually, they would end up in La Jolla, San Diego, where they would rent a place and stay, within walking distance of the ocean, until the summer ended or their money ran out—whichever happened first. It was an unforgettable adventure, opening their eyes to new sights and giving them the freedom to explore. At summer's end, they would board the train for Ontario, back to the classrooms full of young minds that were awaiting them.

The Morning Milking

Bernice Wagler

*The sunrise was barely warming the horizon
as Bernice and her mother crossed the farmyard
and entered the barn. The familiar musky smell of
hay rose to meet them, and in the stalls the cows
lowed their greeting. Just like every morning, they
each milked five cows, then poured the fresh milk
into tall steel cans. They hauled the cans out to
a platform at the end of the lane. Before long,
the milk truck would come to pick it up on its
morning rounds, just as it did every day.*

Bernice Wagler was born on a farm on the 7/8 highway,
now a major thoroughfare between Stratford and Kitchener.
In 1928, it was one of the only paved roads leading out of
town, though there were far fewer cars rushing by in those
days. The construction crew doing the paving had lived in the
farmhouse before Bernice's parents moved in. They used to
throw all their garbage down the cellar stairs, leaving quite a
mess for Bernice' parents to clean up. However, the pavement
made for a smoother ride, especially in the rubber-tired cars
of the 1920s.

Tragedy struck early on when Bernice's father fell ill at
age 35. He had pneumonia, which was a serious threat before the development of penicillin. After nine days of fever
and delirium, he seemed to be past the crisis. The doctor
stopped in at midday and reported that his patient was out
of immediate danger. Relieved, Bernice's mother went outside to plant cucumbers. It was the 24th of May, time to get
them in the ground if she wanted to make pickles later that

Bernice (on her mother's lap) and her family.
The photo was taken by her aunt's hired man,
who owned a camera.

fall. When she finished up in the garden and returned to the house, her husband was dead. They had been married for only nine years. Bernice's mother often remarked that she was grateful to have married when she was only in her teens, so that she had at least that much time with her husband. She never remarried.

Bernice's mother suddenly found herself alone with three young children and another on the way, as well as a large farm to manage. The family rallied under the difficult circumstances. Bernice's grandparents moved to the farmhouse to lend a hand, and they also got a hired man to do the field work. Much of the labour still fell to Bernice, her mother, and her older brother. Some nights, Bernice would stay in her mother's bed, rocking her baby brother to sleep because her mother was too exhausted from the day's work. Then they would each be up at dawn to tend to the morning chores.

The desperation of the Depression was illustrated by an incident when Bernice's home was robbed. Her brothers' piggy banks, containing only a few coins, were stolen from the china cabinet. Luckily, the little glass dish where Bernice kept her coins was passed over by the thief. He also stole a brand new buffalo robe that her grandfather had left draped over the bannister. Money was so tight during those years that Bernice had to wear her brother's shoes to school because there wasn't enough to buy her a new pair. She would walk carefully on the wooden floors so that the cleats on the bottom wouldn't click. At the time, she already felt ostracized because she was the only student without a father—she didn't want anyone knowing that she was wearing boy's shoes on top of that.

Bernice remembers school being very strict. Students did not dare turn around in their desk or talk with their neighbours. Very few people stayed on until grade eight in the farming community, and Bernice was one of only three students in her year to write her entrance exams. When Bernice was in grade eight, Canada was in the midst of the Second World War. With so many young men away, children were needed on the farm during the busy spring season, so instead of going to a larger town to write their exams with a group as they normally would, Bernice and the others were allowed to write the entrance exams early in their classroom, with nobody to answer their questions. Waiting for the results was nerve-wracking, but Bernice eventually got her marks back—she passed!

Bernice's brother, like most of the young men in their Mennonite community, applied for conscientious objector status when the war began, as military service is contrary to the peaceful values of the Mennonite faith. Though they were exempt from fighting, conscientious objectors made other sacrifices as they served their country in non-combatant roles. During the Second World War, there were over 2500 conscientious objectors in Ontario who completed various alternative services across the country, including clearing forests, planting trees, mining, building infrastructure, and working in hospitals. Many of the young men from Bernice's church were sent to Montreal River to work on clearing the Trans-Canada Highway. Bernice's brother was needed on the farm, especially with the added strain of wartime demand. In order to keep him at home, Bernice's mother had to pay the Red Cross $25 a month.

In 1949, Bernice married Laverne Wagler, a friend of her brother's who lived nearby. When Bernice moved out, her mother bought a milking machine to replace her. Bernice continued milking on a dairy farm in North Easthope township, where she raised four daughters and one son. She and her husband still live there today.

The View from the Lighthouse
Lois Bart

The young girl looked at the ingredients before her with a furrowed brow. She picked up the tin of Fry's Cocoa, scrutinizing the recipe printed on its side. She had never baked a cake before, but today, her twelfth birthday, seemed like a good time to try it.

She wrapped her mother's wide apron around her waist and picked up the measuring cups. Flour, sugar, cocoa, and eggs blended together as she worked with ease, stopping periodically to check the recipe on the back of the tin. A few hours later, a rich smell emanated from the oven, and the young girl pulled out the cake. It puffed up over the edges of the cake pan, perfectly baked. Her first foray into baking was a success.

Lois Bart was born a McTaggert, one of Kincardine's significant Scottish community. She spent her first six years there, two blocks away from Lake Huron's sparkling waters. The stately lighthouse which stands at the mouth of the harbour was operated by Lois' great-uncle and aunt. For a week while her parents were away, Lois stayed with them, sleeping in one of the little rooms off the winding circular staircase. The beach was a mainstay in her early childhood. Her grandfather would often take the children down to the shore, where they would help him collect stones for the stone garage that he built in his backyard. They happily filled many wagon loads with big smooth stones.

Some of Lois's fondest memories of Kincardine are of campfires on the beach with her family, roasting marshmal-

The Kincardine lighthouse.

lows and wieners with the soft splash of waves in the background. The children were never allowed to go down to the beach alone, because the road to get there crossed beneath a railway tunnel. During the Depression, transients would often gather under the bridge or in the woods nearby since Kincardine was the last stop on the rail line.

Lois's father struggled to find a steady job during the thirties. He would set out each morning to pick up loads of fish down at the docks and sell them door-to-door through the city. On one particularly tight Christmas, the Salvation Army delivered a basket of food and a small parcel of gifts to the family. Lois was greatly disappointed when the adorable black patent shoes they left for her were a size too small. She had to give them away to her aunt. Eventually, the family moved to Shawinigan Falls, Quebec, where Lois' father found work in a cellophane factory. There, Lois learned French and promptly forgot how to speak English. That Christmas, they decorated their tree with the coloured scraps from the factory which they fashioned into icicle decorations.

Lois's father answered an ad in the paper to become a train engineer on the CNR, a job which became his life's work. Lois would sometimes accompany him when he drove the train between Kincardine and Stratford, arriving at her destination covered in coal soot. An engineer's life was a mobile one, and the family moved to several Ontario towns.

When Lois was ten, they arrived in Stratford. Lois's first impressions of the city were not favourable. However, she soon discovered there was lots of fun to be had in the town. Several evenings a week, a roller rink would be made by closing off the street from the YMCA to the corner of St. Patrick Street, allowing kids to practice their figure eights without fear of traffic. Lois's family had only one pair of roller skates among five children, so there was always some squabbling on those evenings. Sometimes, she would end up spinning around the rink with only one skate.

After finishing school, Lois got a job working alongside her mother at Grosch Felt Shoe Factory. The entire shoe was made at that factory—first it was sewn, fitted with stiff stays to maintain its shape, and then tacked onto a sole. Lois's department was the last stop in the assembly of the shoe. She made and stacked the shoe boxes, while her mother painted the sole and packed the shoes, two by two, in their boxes. They were then shipped away in big cartons.

One evening, Lois was riding home from an open-air dance in the rumble seat of her friend's Model A Ford. There was a car accident up ahead, so they pulled the car over, and all the passengers went to investigate except Lois. She stayed behind in the rumble seat, leaving an opportunity for one of the boys to come back and introduce himself. He asked her for a date, and soon they were going steady. In those days, a typical date consisted of going downtown for a Coke or catching a show at the movie theatre. On Sunday evenings, they sometimes went to Rankin's for a sundae. Lois's father was transferredw to Palmerston when she was in her teens, but this time she remained in Stratford. She already had a job, and her relationship was becoming serious.

Lois and her husband in 1942.

After two years of dating, Lois and her boyfriend decided to get married. She went downtown to Greenberg's Dress Shop on Ontario Street to pick out her wedding dress. "You were somebody if you could buy a dress from Greenberg's," she recalls. The long white satin dress with French Illusion lace panels that she chose cost $50. She paid for it herself in weekly installments of $2. Her wedding was held at 9 a.m., followed by a reception brunch prepared by her mother-in-law. At 4 p.m., she donned her going-away dress (also purchased from Greenberg's), and the newlyweds set off by bus for their honeymoon in Toronto. The morning had been unseasonably warm for November, but by the time they departed it was snowing.

It was the beginning of a happy 56-year marriage which were blessed with four children. In 1970, Lois's husband fulfilled his dream of living on a farm when they moved to a

169

Lois and her children in their Easter bonnets.

country property near Brunner. Lois worked at a dry cleaning centre in Stratford but returned each evening to the farm, where she and her husband raised animals and tended large gardens of organic vegetables. She returned to Stratford upon her retirement, putting her free time to good use on many baking projects.

The Only Lady in the Lab
Doris Ley

Doris walked confidently into the metallurgical laboratory of Cockshutt Farm Equipment, her new workplace. It was a brand new lab, divided into rooms by glass partitions and outfitted with the most advanced technology. As she entered the chemistry room, the light glinted off the gleaming stainless steel fume hood. This was where she would be working, running chemical tests for the various products that Cockshutt was manufacturing.

At first, her presence elicited a few raised eyebrows from the men in the laboratory. There had been two women in the position before her, but neither had been able to do the work. Doris was determined to prove herself. She was a farm girl through and through, so a little dirt and heavy lifting would not put her off. More importantly, she was a quick and willing learner.

"Doris, this is the procedure," the chief metallurgist said, dropping a thick book onto the lab bench. Doris nodded, opened the first page, and began reading. It was the beginning of a noteworthy career as North America's first female metallurgy technologist.

In the heart of tobacco country near Otterville, Doris Ley was born in the year 1916. Her father died very early of pneumonia, so her older brother shouldered the responsibility of running two dairy farms at the young age of eighteen. Doris,

171

too, took on men's work, lending a hand in the field and the barns. Growing up in the middle of an Irish settlement, "we would dance til two in the morning, then get up at five to milk the cows!"

In her one-room schoolhouse, all the grades' lessons were written on the board at once, so Doris often worked ahead. As a result, she skipped two grades and started high school at age ten. By the time she graduated, the family had been plunged into the economic hardship of the Depression. There was no money to send her to teachers' college, so she returned to the farm. She married a local tobacco buyer and had one son, who spent most of his childhood at Sick Kids Hospital as a result of complications at his birth. Her marriage dissolved, and Doris went to Brantford looking for work.

It was at Cockshutt Farm Equipment that she found her calling. During her interview, the Public Relations manager asked her what she was interested in. She replied that she had always enjoyed science and math in high school. They offered her a position in the metallurgical lab, and she accepted. It was April 1943, and she would spend the next eighteen years working there. At the time, there were no spectrometers; all chemical testing was done 'the hard way' by dissolving materials in acids, using titration, precipitate, carbon trains, sulfur emissions, and other methods.

Wartime necessity had replaced tractors with aircrafts on the Cockshutt production line, so much of Doris's early work was with the undercarriage of the Lancaster bomber. For her first two weeks on the job, Doris worked with a hardness tester and a grinding stone, checking the forgings. Later, Doris would test samples from the undercarriage, cutting them in half and etching them in acid to examine the grain flow. The undercarriage was extremely important, since the 'Lanc' carried 8000 lb. bombs, the heaviest in the European theatre. They were sent to Malton, Ontario for assembly.

Another war material manufactured by Cockshutt was

track pins for tanks. These pins fit interchangeably in British, American, and Canadian tank tracks, making repair on the battlefield much easier. Doris ran multiple microscopic, chemical, and physical tests on these pins. She also used cyanide salt baths to test the percent strength for heat-treating the pins. This was a dangerous job, given the reactivity of cyanide and water. If any moisture got into the cyanide, it would cause an explosion that sent molten cyanide flying into the air.

Another important part of Doris's job was running tests for the factory's five boilers, which produced steam to heat and power all the factory buildings. Those boiler rooms were so loud, engineers had to take breaks in a noise-protected office every fifteen minutes. Each day, the stationary engineers would bring back water samples, which Doris would analyse to check that the additives to prevent lime and corrosive-material buildup were in their correct proportion. The additives were supplied by Dearborn Chemical of Toronto, and Doris came to know the chemist there well.

The Dearborn chemist also supplied additives to a nearby glue factory on the edge of Brantford. He trusted Doris so much that when he doubted the results he was receiving from the glue factory, he would call her.

"Are you busy tonight, Doris?" he would ask, and she would come in after hours to run the tests on the glue factory samples, just to help him out.

Doris speaks highly of the men she worked with. Many were brilliant scientists and engineers, eminent in their fields. However, one of her most memorable colleagues was a young woman who worked under her as a technician. She was "quite a whiz," fresh out of high school when she came to the lab for metallurgical training. She and Doris worked together seamlessly and efficiently; they really had a rhythm. They would never go to the cafeteria together for lunch, because there was always something cooking in the lab that needed to be supervised. Visitors would remark that they had never seen anyone run as many tests in one day as those two. Amidst all the work, they found time to kid each other about the handsome new man in the lab, an American engineer who had arrived to set up the factory's new automatic foundry.

"He's so handsome," the girl gushed.

Doris scoffed in reply. "He's old enough to be your father."

It turned out that the engineer had his eye on Doris as well. On his last day in the plant, he asked her out on a date. They had much in common, but in the end, Doris decided that she couldn't marry him.

She couldn't imagine waiting all day in a swanky hotel for him to come home, without any interesting work of her own. Her farm upbringing had imbued in her the value of hard work, while her metallurgical experience had ignited her passion for science.

Doris and the engineer celebrating New Year's Eve.

When Cockshutt unrolled the world's first automatic combine, it brought changes to the company. Cockshutt was bought out by White Motor and moved to the United States.

Doris decided that it was time for a move as well, so she took a job with SKF, the Swedish ball bearing manufacturer. Her career in metallurgy continued to grow from there. After SKF, she worked at Pratt and Whitney on aircraft bearings. She came out of retirement to help Monroe Automotive set up their metallurgy laboratory and train technicians for manufacturing piston rods. Once the 'only gal' in the Cockshutt lab, Doris retired forty years later a widely-known and well-respected metallurgy technologist who had proved that there was a place for women in the field.

Doris in the SKF laboratory.

The Runaway Milk Cart
Jerry Richards

Jerry was just finishing his morning coffee at the service station beside the Queen's Hotel when he heard a terrible clatter and the sound of a horse galloping up Ontario Street. It was the early 1950s, and cars had long since replaced horse-drawn wagons on area roads—all except for the milk wagon. Every morning, Jerry was accustomed to hearing the clip-clop of horses' hooves down the driveway of Silverwoods Dairy two doors down, but he had never heard them gallop with quite this speed before!

"What on earth is that driver doing?" he wondered. The horse showed no sign of slowing down, though he had nearly reached the dairy.

Jerry stepped out of the shop in time to see the horse stop suddenly, skidding on all four legs as the wagon's momentum pushed it forward. It turned sharply into the driveway and the buggy jumped the curb behind it, sending two crates of empty milk bottles smashing to the sidewalk. Finally the horse came to a stop, pinned into the corner by the buggy.

After a moment, Jerry heard a jingling sound from the alleyway. It was the change in the milk-man's purse as he came puffing into view. They shared a look of shock—whatever spooked that horse on its morning rounds had certainly caused a ruckus.

When Jerry Richards was born, his parents owned a grocery transport trucking company in Stratford. In those days, there were no 18-wheelers trundling down the road with 50 foot trailers; instead, the Richards delivered their sacks of salt and barrels of vinegar in an open-backed pick-up truck with hard rubber tires. Business was tense during the Depression years, and the stress wore on Jerry's father. The doctor told him, "You can either stay in business and quit worrying about it, or get rid of it. If you don't, we'll all be going to your funeral soon."

They eventually exchanged the trucking business for a farm, but the stress did not diminish. At a time when farmers were making very little money, there was no way to keep up with mortgage payments. Instead, Jerry's father went to work for other farmers. One of the farms was only a half-mile from Lake Erie, so the kids would run down to the beach after the evening chores were done to cool off and splash in the waves. The family finally settled in Ethel, a small town in Huron County, where Jerry's dad operated a garage and farm equipment store.

Throughout his childhood, Jerry made frequent visits to Stratford, where much of his family still resided. He recalls swimming in the Avon River with his cousins and going to see the show with his Uncle Dave at the Theatre Albert, where the Avon Theatre stands today. They always entered the theatre halfway through the first showing, and stayed to catch the movie again on its second showing of the evening.

One ambitious day, Jerry and his cousin biked from Ethel to Listowel, a 22 km journey, then decided to continue on to Stratford. The 50 km trip was uneventful until they reached the outskirts of town, when the pedal fell off Jerry's bike. Nevertheless, they forged onwards. Finally nearing their destination on Ontario Street, Jerry's cousin was hit by a car, knocking him off his bike onto the sidewalk. After their long ride, the rest of the day was spent at the hospital treating a greenstick fracture in his shoulder.

In 1956, the family moved to Stratford for good, to be closer to family after Jerry's father's death. There, Jerry worked for and eventually ran the Shell Station on Ontario Street near Silverwoods Dairy. At that time, the city sustained six different dairies at once, each of which delivered to a different section of the city. They all still used the outmoded horse-and-wagon transportation because of the convenience—the horse knew its route so well that the driver could hop off with his carrier of six bottles and service two or three houses while his horse carried on down the street, stopping when he reached the end. It was much more convenient than parking a truck at each stop.

Silverwoods kept six horses stabled behind the dairy on Albert Street. Every morning except Sunday, they would set off, each horse and driver covering a certain route through the city. At the time, people left their empty bottle and money for the milkman on the front porch or in the milk box near the side door. The milkman would simply exchange the bottles and carry on. It all went smoothly most of the time, but on rare occasions the horse would spook and head for the stables with no care for its fragile load, as it did that memorable day on Ontario Street.

Many years later, Jerry still remembers the shock on the milkman's face when he finally caught up to his runaway cart.

On the Shores of the Avon
Jean Dawson

The booming tuba could be heard first, followed by the patter of the snare drum as the band members marched from their practice rooms above Northways store to the band shell on the banks of the Avon. It was a Wednesday night, and crowds of Stratford citizens had turned out for the weekly Boys' Band Concert. The river was truly the place to be on summer evenings in the late 1930s. After the concert, families would go for walks around the river, and couples would rent canoes from the boathouse. If the evening was humid, kids would splash in the waters at the beach, which was shaded by willow trees near the dam. Back then, the water was clear enough to see every rock on the bottom.

Jean stood with the other young ladies on the sidewalk, watching as the band rounded the corner playing their jaunty melody. She always stood on the same side of the street, because it was the side on which the handsome drummer passed. She caught a glimpse of him as he went by, his face concentrated, and his hands moving swiftly. Someday, she vowed, she would work up the courage to talk to him.

Like many others, Jean's father came to Stratford to work for the Canadian National Railroad. One day, he returned from work early with his face completely bandaged. He had been burned in an explosion, ending his career as an engineer.

Next, he went to work for Stratford's other major industry at the time, the furniture factories. Many of Jean's toys were handmade by him from wood scraps that he brought home. She especially loved the wagon he made for her dolls. When she was three, Jean set off downtown with her baby brother in the wagon, clutching a handful of buttons to buy some candy. Fortunately, her mother caught up with her a few blocks into the journey.

Jean and her brother.

One summer, the family decided to go to Bayfield in her uncle's new Model T Ford. The backseat was so spacious that they could fit a little kiddie chair for Jean in between the front and the back seats. They got a flat tire at the first stop sign, but that didn't deter the beach-bound travellers. They stuffed the tire with leaves and dried grass until it was full. That took them all the way to Bayfield and back—though it was a rather bumpy trip.

Jean and her brother Ken spent most of their playtime outdoors, but each time the train whistle blew, her mother would call them inside. The family lived near the railroad tracks, and each train that stopped brought 'tramps' looking for work. Jean's house was known as a friendly place for hungry men, so they would frequently come knocking. Her mother always gave them a sandwich to eat on the porch but insisted that the children stay inside.

For a young girl, the dreariness of the Depression was mitigated by simple pleasures. After Jean's father lost his job, the family had to go on welfare. This was a great embarrassment to her mother, but Jean was thrilled! She was accustomed to wearing clothes from the rummage sale which her mother would alter, but the welfare coupons provided new fabric for the family. For the first time, Jean got to wear a dress made of brand-new material. She also remembers the entertainment which the City of Stratford would host to lift people's spirits during the Depression. There was a fair held in the Brooks Steam Motors factory on Ontario Street. It included free music, entertainment, and a chance for families to forget about their troubles and enjoy the company of neighbours. Jean and her brother were particularly excited about the magician at the event.

Eventually, Jean's father got a job building the highway between Gadshill and Topping. It was one of many public works projects that the government sponsored to provide work to able-bodied men during the Depression. Everyday at sun-up, he would be picked up at the end of their street in a truck with the other men. They would work all day beneath the baking sun and were dropped off at home as the sun was sinking behind the trees. It was a hard job, but it carried the family through the toughest years.

The highlight of Jean's school days was learning the Maypole dance to perform in the park on the first of May. They had practiced inside all winter to prepare. After school, she spent hours in her backyard on the trapeze her father had made her, practicing her acrobatic tricks.

Jean was fifteen when she met the young man who would become her husband. She had long admired him from the audience of the Boys' Band concerts, so one Wednesday night she asked her cousin's boyfriend to introduce them. He went up to the front and began motioning for the drummer to come meet them after the concert, flustering him so much that he missed his drum solo. After the concert, he walked Jean home through the humid summer air. They spent a lot of time walking and talking. Four years later, they married.

Jean's husband, in his Boys' Band uniform.

During the Second World War, Jean and her mother were left at home alone with their dog, Tiny. Her father worked in an Air Force hospital in Toronto, and her brother Ken served overseas in the Navy. Jean, her mom, and Tiny slept in the same bed all week until Friday night, when Jean's father would arrive home on the late train. When he got in after the long train trip, Tiny would growl and bark, unwilling to give up his place in bed to this new arrival. He wouldn't stop until Jean's mother told him off, laughing.

One wartime shortage which caused amusement was the

lack of rubber. It wasn't until there was no rubber that everyone realized how useful it was—especially as an elastic waistband for underwear. Without elastic, they had to sew buttons on their underwear. Many considered it a great joke when those buttons would pop off unexpectedly.

Jean's husband wasn't able to enlist for health reasons, but he played an important role at home as a firefighter. The two were living in an apartment downtown when the war ended. Jean climbed out onto the roof of the ice cream store beside her and watched the crowds of people down below celebrating VE Day. The cars which passed could hardly be seen because there were so many people hanging off them, sitting on the hood and on the trunk. Several weeks afterwards, Jean was in the midst of her laundry when the telephone rang.

"Ken's coming home on the next train," her mother said. Jean turned off the taps and ran from downtown Stratford to her parent's home on the outskirts of town. She arrived breathless at the door just as her brother arrived, in time to wrap him in an enormous hug. Life could finally return to normal.

Later, Jean and her husband settled in a house on Water Street. They raised five children there, a stone's throw away from the Avon River.

Jean's wedding.

Social Work Across the World
Cliff Taylor

Cliff pushed open the door to his Edmonton apartment, cradling a six-month-old baby in his arms. It was 10 p.m., and he had just flown in from Whitehorse where he'd been called to visit a young Air Force man in distress. Cliff found him at his wit's end; his wife had recently left him, wanting nothing more to do with him or their newborn baby. He had no idea how to look after a baby and juggle his Air Force duties at the same time. Fortunately, the child's grandparents lived in Edmonton, where Cliff also resided with his wife and two children. As leader of the Royal Canadian Air Force's fledgling social work program, he was accustomed to addressing a wide range of problems—though transporting a baby by plane from the Yukon to Alberta was hardly in his job description.

Nevertheless, Cliff and his wife did not hesitate. They fashioned a crib out of a dresser drawer and some blankets, and settled the baby in for the night. The reunion between the baby and his grandparents the next morning was a joyful one for all involved.

Cliff Taylor's involvement with the Royal Canadian Air Force began with the outbreak of the Second World War. Newly married and living in northern British Columbia, Cliff joined up and spent the first years of the war as a flight instructor at air bases in Western Ontario. Then, he was sent

184

overseas to pilot Mosquito bombers on their night missions over Europe. After VE Day, he came home on leave, expecting to be sent to the Pacific theatre next. On a train crossing the Prairies, he got word that the Japanese had capitulated; he was coming home for good.

Cliff in the cockpit.

After a short stay on his parent's dairy farm outside of Chilliwack, Cliff returned to Vancouver to be released from the Air Force. While his paperwork was being completed, an officer asked him if he'd ever thought of returning to school. The government was offering education to veterans to help them re-adjust to civilian life.

"I would have liked to," he replied, "but I grew up in northern Saskatchewan where the school only went to grade ten." He'd long ago given up the idea of obtaining entrance to university.

The officer presented him with a proposal: there was a course being held in Vancouver that covered grade nine, ten, eleven, and twelve in only six months. It was very intensive, but those who could make it through would have no trouble gaining entrance to university.

Intrigued, Cliff went home to discuss it with his wife. They decided to move to Vancouver with their two children, and Cliff began the high school equivalency course. Following that, he studied biochemistry, intending to go to medical school. However, the interruption of the war had left a huge backlog of medical students, leaving no spaces for new students to be accepted that year. They offered Cliff a place the following year, but with two children at home, he couldn't prolong his education further. Instead, he went into social work, specializing in psychiatrics. Much of his training was done in a 5000 bed mental health facility outside of Vancouver. Cliff would return home to his busy household exhausted after the day's instruction.

Cliff and his wife Joan in 1942.

At the time, there was a great demand for social workers in North America, and graduates were given a book listing vacant positions to which they could apply. Cliff and his wife were considering a position in Hawaii when the Air Force unexpectedly summoned him. They were way behind in schedule and wanted him to fly for them again. Cliff turned down the offer. "I hadn't gone to school for six years just to get back behind the wheel of a plane."

Undeterred, the sergeant asked Cliff what he had studied and presented him with another offer. The Air Force was just beginning to establish a social work program to support RCAF members with family and personal issues. This was an opportunity Cliff could not pass up. He rejoined the Air Force and continued his career with them as a social worker.

Even in his new position as social worker for Alberta, British Columbia, and the Yukon, he still found himself in the air frequently. He would take a plane out to remote calls or catch a ride with a plane that was already going where he was needed. After several years, he was promoted to oversee all social work at the Canadian Air Force's European and Middle Eastern bases. This required him to move to Metz, France with his growing family.

Cliff coordinated the efforts of three social workers under him who provided service to troops in Greece, Turkey, Saudi Arabia, Italy, Germany, England, and France. During the '50s, Canadian peacekeepers were active in Egypt, causing Cliff to visit the army base in the desert outside of Jerusalem nine times. When he was there, he couldn't wear his customary officer's hat, instead donning the light blue beret worn by United Nations forces. After three years, another promotion brought him back to Ottawa. He spent six years there as the head of the social service program for the entire Canadian military.

Having served for 20 years with the Air Force, Cliff decided it was time for a change. He and his family made one last move—to Stratford. Here, he served as director of the Perth County Children's Aid Society for fifteen years.

The Black Cherry Tree

Roy Miller

It was a hot, muggy day in late August, and the boughs of the cherry trees hung heavy with shiny, glistening fruit. The thickly knotted branches stretched across the sky. They had been there for as long as anyone could remember. Even the neighbour lady, who had spent ninety years on the farm next to theirs, could not recall a time when those trees weren't as tall as they were then. In all those years, there had never before been a harvest like this one.

The young boy lifted his smaller sister up so that she could reach the higher branches. The cherries dropped into the basket with a quiet thud, filling it quickly. They set the full basket near the others. Over the course of the tree's short season, they would fill 75 eleven-quart baskets and sell them at the market for 50 cents apiece. All winter long, the taste of canned black cherries was preserved in the shiny glass jars lined up neatly in the fruit cellar, a lingering memory of the summer's bounty.

When Roy Miller was young, he lived on a small farm near Harrington. His father had moved the family from Stratford shortly after Roy's birth, wanting to set his son up with some land. However, the hard times of the Depression made mortgage payments difficult, and soon the family had to give up their first farm near Gadshill and move to a smaller one. It was hardly enough to make a living on, and money was always short. However, for Roy, it was home.

The farmhouse, like many at that time, was a simple log house covered in boards. On visits to town as a boy, Roy would marvel at the ease of flipping a switch and seeing a light come on across the room. Electricity was installed in his own home when he was 16. Telephone service was another new technology that brought excitement to the household when he was growing up. In those days, you had to wait until enough people on your road wanted a telephone before you could get service. Two long rings and one short was the number which reached Roy's house—but with 20 other neighbours all sharing the same phone line, you could count on your conversations being overheard far and wide. Covering the mouthpiece and listening in was a common form of entertainment for the isolated rural-dweller. If you had a talkative neighbour, it was hard to get your calls in edgewise!

Even during the lean years of the Depression, the Millers were never in want of food. There were always potatoes, cabbages, and turnips to tide the family over through the winter until the garden produce became plentiful again. The family kept pigs, cows, and a few chickens, so they were supplied with milk, eggs, and meat. Days were spent ploughing, harvesting, and working in the fields. Come the evening, neighbours and friends would gather to visit, deal out a few rounds of euchre, or play crokinole. The neighbourhood boys played softball in the summer months.

One of the biggest farm jobs was the yearly threshing, which took place in the fall after harvest. Threshing is the process of separating the edible grain from the inedible chaff that surrounds it. In the days before combines, this was accomplished by the threshing machine, a lumbering piece of equipment which went from farm to farm, accompanied by a team of fifteen to eighteen men from the neighbourhood. The farmers would trade back and forth, each working on each other's farms until the work was done, never keeping track of how long they spent at each place. The big event of the

Roy, on his neighbour's tractor.

threshing day was the midday meal, prepared by the lady of the house for the whole team. It became a friendly competition among the neighbour ladies to see who could furnish the heartiest meal finished off with the most delectable pies and cakes to fuel the men through the rest of their day. At threshing time, they would often stay in the fields until dusk only to return to their own barns where the cows were waiting to be milked and chores needing to be done. Roy's first job was working on the threshing team, tramping the straw stack. For this, he was paid a princely 75 cents a day. Years later, the man who employed him ended up becoming his future father-in-law.

When Roy married and had a family of his own, it was time to move into Stratford. The farm simply wasn't big enough to support four children. Roy got a job first as a guard at the local jail and later as an elementary school custodian, never returning to rural life. However, whenever he drives past fields of wheat or other crops, he's reminded of his upbringing on the farm.

Joined in Thought and Prayer
Marj Gibson

At first, it seemed to be an ordinary day. Marj and her mother were doing the laundry, a weekly chore which took most of the morning. For weeks, the people of Stratford had been glued to their radios. The rumours had been growing about an upcoming invasion into Europe, a big push that might turn the tide of the war. After five years, everyone was hoping for something to break the stalemate and hasten the return of their boys. At 10 a.m., the factory whistles across town blew, and the church bells rang. That was the signal— the boys were going into France.

Marj's mother hurried to the church still wearing her pinny and started to play the piano as the people filed in. Shopkeepers came with their sleeves still rolled up to their elbows. Children came, holding tightly to their mothers' hands with their knees still sandy from the sandbox. Men from Kroehler's and Avalon Fabrics streamed out of the factories and slid into the pews with their overalls still on. Mr. Chesterpratt got to the church before the preacher did, so he got behind the pulpit and began leading the congregation in prayer.

Seated beside her father, Marj looked around at the faces of her neighbours. Some were joyful, others drawn with worry, others sad. All were joined together in one common, fervent prayer. Across the ocean, men were climbing out of boats onto the beaches of Normandy and fighting for their lives. Some fell and never rose again, while the others pushed onwards against terrible odds. The people of Stratford, though far away in body, were right behind them in spirit.

Marj Gibson was only thirteen when the Second World War began. She recalls lying awake at night worrying when her friends' fathers had to leave for the war. As brothers and fathers departed for training camps, families would grow accustomed to setting out one less dinner plate each evening. At Marj's table, however, she had to remind herself to set out four extra plates. When the Perth Regiment began to assemble in Stratford in 1939, the government barracks on Duoro Street were not yet completed. Marj's family, like many local homes, took in soldiers as boarders. Marj's mother often remarked that the money she made from boarding soldiers was the first $1000 she had ever made. The Depression was still fresh in their memories, and the family was not accustomed to having excess money.

A parade through the streets of Stratford.

On the first day of the boarders' stay, the youngest one, Vern, made quite an impression. First he fell down the stairs, and then he spilled the ketchup at the dinner table. Soon his clumsiness became endearing, and the family grew to love his energetic, friendly nature. He became such a close friend that he even took Marj and her friend to the fair. Even when the barracks were finished and the boarders moved out, Vern continued to spend time with the family. He had left his wife and baby son in Barrie when he joined up, so he enjoyed having a home away from home.

Marj and Toby in front of the Preston-Noelting Furniture Factory.

For a young girl, the Perth Regiment's training brought some excitement to the town. The barracks were just down the street from Marj's home, and the troops would parade by every day. She remembers standing on the front lawn watching them go by and cheering them on. They were always accompanied by their mascot, a dog named Toby who was named after the regiment's colonel. When they left Stratford, nearly the whole town came to the train station at 11 p.m. to see them off. The atmosphere was uneasy—nobody knew where the regiment was being sent or what they would find when they got there.

The Perth Regiment's absence was soon filled by Dutch soldiers who came to train in Stratford. They were housed in

McLagan's Furniture Factory, and Marj would watch them doing their drills in the schoolyard of Juliet. Some evenings, they would come in for ice cream and sweets at Rankin's, where Marj had a part-time job. They hung around the store a lot because one of the Dutch boys was dating Marj's co-worker. Marj herself was never allowed to join them at the Blue Room dance hall uptown. "My parents wouldn't let me go unless my dad came with me," Marj recalls. "So of course, I wouldn't go." The soldiers brought a jovial atmosphere with them, and they were warmly welcomed into the community.

Marj and Vern in the front yard.

Over time, the sadness of the war began to weigh on the people of Stratford. Marj became accustomed to watching the telegraph boy come down her street on his bike. She would stay out on the porch to watch which house he was going into, knowing that he carried bad news for that family. She wrote letters to Vern, who had been sent to Italy to serve as a motorcycle dispatcher. One day, Marj's letter was returned to her, the envelope edged in black. With a sinking feeling, she realized that Vern had been killed. She sent her condolences to his wife, beginning a correspondence that continues to this day.

A Christmas card from Vern, which reads "I think of you, Marj, Ma, and Gordon. Best wishes, Vern."

In the face of hardship, the Stratford community pulled together. Women stepped in to fill men's roles, not only in the factories and on the farm but also in community life. Usually men ran the Scouts Service, but women took over in their absence. Marj rose to be a Cub Leader when she was still only a teenager. The Red Cross rooms in the Market Square were always full of local women, knitting or making hospital pads to be sent overseas. Townspeople offered support in any way they could—and when the war finally came to an end, they all turned out for the celebrations.

The Clicking of Keys
Doreen Alexander

The young women sat across from each other, their fingers poised above identical Underwood typewriters. Another woman stood above them, her eyes fixed on the clock. "Ready... and... start!"

With a clatter, they started to type. The machines shook with the force of their flying fingers, and the office was filled with the "clackety-clack" of keys striking paper. The two women were accustomed to typing on carbon paper, where one false key meant they had to rip out the whole page and start again, so their movements were precise. Their fingers were a blur as the second hand rounded the nine. Finally— "Stop!"

Laughing, both women pulled out their sheets and handed them over. After a few moments, the timekeeper returned her verdict. "It was a close race. Doreen, you typed 102 words per minute." She turned to the other woman. "And our champion, with 106 words per minute!"

After some good-natured laughter, they turned back to their typewriters and fed in new carbon sheets. Until the next slow afternoon, Doreen would have to content herself with being the second-best typist in Kroehler's stenography department.

Doreen Alexander grew up on Huron Street at the edge of Stratford. Her memories of those times are happy ones; she recalls sitting on the front porch with her Dad watching summer storms roll through the city and spending Sunday afternoons playing with a crowd of cousins at her grandparents' farm. Whenever the ice truck delivered on their street, she and her siblings would chase after it and pick up the little pieces of ice it dropped, to suck on. They had no freezer at home, so ice was a novelty!

Doreen attended Avon Public school, which was quite strict in those days. In the wintertime, her teachers would check to make sure students were dressed in their long wool stockings and garters. If they weren't, they'd be sent home with a note. The stockings were itchy and always slipping, so Doreen and her sister couldn't wait to banish them to the back of the closet in the spring. After Doreen's birthday in April, their mother permitted them to leave the garters behind, which they did no matter how cold it was outside. In high school, fashion started to become more important. Poodle skirts with crinolines and saddle shoes with ankle socks were all the rage. Hats, too, were a much more integral accessory than they are today. No lady would venture into church without her hat and gloves. Each Easter, Doreen's mother took her to the milliner's shop on Downie Street to buy a new wide-brimmed hat for the season.

Doreen always had a job growing up, whether it was scooping ice cream at the local parlour or helping customers at the grocery store. After her last year of high school, she enrolled in the Special Commercial program, in which students learned typing, shorthand, and book-keeping as well as other administrative skills. Special Commercial students were in high demand, and employers would come directly to the high school to interview them for positions. Doreen was hired on at G.L. Griffith's for $35 a week. Soon, her friends at Kroehler's Furniture Factory alerted her to an opening for a clerk, and she got the job there. Later, she moved into the stenography department. At the time, Kroehler's was a booming factory, shipping furniture across North America. In its heydey, it was one of the city's largest employers, along with the CNR shops.

Spring and Fall were the busiest times in the office, because that was when Kroehler's unveiled their new furniture collections for the season. Doreen and the other office girls worked overtime typing the descriptions of each piece for the furniture shows across Canada where they would exhibit their wares. The best part of the job was the friendships among the office girls. They made a sport of teasing their good-natured office manager, who would hurry out of his office waving a pencil to scold them if there was too much chatter. Unfazed, they would pull the pencil out of his fingers and carry on. They always found a way to infuse their day with fun.

When summer came around, the office gals would rent a cottage together in Port Elgin for their vacation, spending their days on the beach and their nights at the big band dance halls. The yearly office parties were another highlight. There were always games, food, and music to entertain the thirty office workers. At Christmas, the entire factory would gather for a party, which was an even splashier affair. At one, Doreen and a few co-workers performed the Charleston up on stage.

After eight years at Kroehler's, Doreen married and moved to Clinton. In the years since, Kroehler's has closed down and the Arden Park Hotel has gone up in its place, reflecting the transition from manufacturing to tourism that the town has undergone. Doreen, too, has changed with the times, trading her typewriter for a computer keyboard. She is still a speedy typist.

Doreen and her sister, Marlene.

Experiencing Ethiopia
Hoda Rushdy

It was dinnertime, but Hoda Rushdy and her family sat in darkness at their kitchen table. Their electricity had been off for days now as the fighting raged in the street below. It was Ethiopia in the year 1960, and the country was torn by a coup which sought to overthrow Emperor Selassie. In the streets, the Imperial Guard was fighting the army and police forces. The Rushdys were distressed to learn that their house was located right in the midst of the army's ammunition stores, so they were unwittingly caught in the middle of the fracas.

Suddenly, a bazooka shell tore through the ceiling, smashed into the floor, and shattered. A piece of shrapnel hit Hoda's son in the back of his neck. Fortunately, it did not lodge itself in his neck, but rather skimmed across and back out. Dinner was abandoned as Hoda rushed to stop the bleeding and comfort her screaming children. The Rushdys retreated with their neighbours to a small room beneath the stairs, which they padded with mats and mattresses. They waited out the coup there, until Emperor Selassie was restored to power and order returned.

When it was finally safe to emerge, Hoda's son found himself to be a local celebrity. Their Ethiopian neighbours would come to the garden gate, asking to see the boy who had been shot. He would trot out proudly, presenting his t-shirt with

the holes from the shrapnel for his audience. Hoda
watched from the window, overwhelmed with re-
lief and gratitude that he was safe, after such an
intense brush with danger.

Hoda Rushdy was born in a city in Upper Egypt. Her father was the Inspector of Arts for the Ministry of Education, and every two years, he would be sent to another province of Egypt. They were living in Alexandria when the Second World War began, and they soon became embroiled in the conflict. Six-year-old Hoda and her brothers became accustomed to hurrying downstairs to the air raid shelters with gas masks in hand. Often the raids would last from the afternoon until the following morning. El Alamein, a small town just over the hill from Alexandria, was the site of several major battles between the Allied and Axis powers.

As the war worsened, Hoda's father decided to move the family to a smaller village, protected from the threat of bombings. Later, they returned to Alexandria to visit relatives. While they were there, they stopped in at the home of a close family friend. Sparks flew between Hoda and their son, and the two married when Hoda was eighteen. Both families were members of the Baha'i faith, a quickly-growing religious community which emphasizes the unity of humankind and believes that all major religions come from the same spiritual source. Their union was considered to be a blessed one by both families.

The Baha'i Faith has no clergy or missionaries, but when there is a need for communities to be built, members volunteer to go, securing their own livelihood and paying their own way. When Hoda and her husband heard that there was a need for Baha'i community development in parts of Africa, they felt compelled to go. With their two-year-old daughter in tow, they packed up and moved to Ethiopia.

Hoda looks back on their years in Ethiopia as a remarkable time in their life. She and her husband were like sponges,

Hoda wearing a traditional Ethiopian dress.

soaking up the new culture and language and tackling each challenge with youthful enthusiasm and vigor. Life in Africa was more primitive than they had been used to, but they felt at home immediately thanks to the warmth of the Ethiopian people. Hoda was impressed by their dignity and rich traditions and touched by their eagerness to teach her the local language. It sounded musical to her ears, and she was able to pick it up within a year.

The capital of Ethiopia was a sprawling, bustling city. It was home to many foreigners, so it was not uncommon to hear a handful of different languages all being spoken on the main street. There was a large Italian presence in the country because of its initial colonization by Italy, as well as considerable Dutch, German, and Greek populations. Many hotel owners and shop-keepers—as well as the family next door—spoke Italian, so Hoda soon learned their language as well. When her young children reached school age, they attended a French school. With her children and husband speaking French, Hoda did not want to be left out, so she took evening conversation classes at the school. Soon, she was fluent in that language in addition to her mother tongue, Arabic, which they always spoke at home. The Rushdys stayed in Ethiopia for eleven-and-a-half years, leaving behind a flourishing Baha'i community, as well as many life-long friends.

Serving chiffon cakes at the Baha'i Festival of Ridvan.

When it came time to leave, the Rushdys did not consider returning to Egypt. The Egyptian government at the time was very intolerant to the Baha'i religion, because its holy grounds and the Baha'i World Centre are located in Haifa, Israel. Though they have no connection to Israel, the intense conflict between Israel and Egypt prevents understanding. Even abroad, the Egyptian embassy confiscated Hoda and her husband's passports, so they had to obtain *laissez-passer* from the United Nations in order to travel. Their journeys took then to Uganda and Kenya, and finally to Burundi in Central Africa, where they spent twenty-three years. Unlike in Ethiopia, the Burundi people did not encourage foreigners to learn their language, preferring to keep it to themselves. Though she took language lessons, that was one language that Hoda never did master.

Her multilingualism proved to be an asset when she moved with her husband to England, where they had been asked to establish an Office for Arab Affairs for the Baha'i World Centre. There was a lot of work to be done there. They were desperate for someone to translate all the reports and correspondence from Arab-speaking countries to English. Always willing, Hoda volunteered her translating skills for 17 years. In 2001, two years after her husband's passing, she crossed the ocean to be nearer to her children in Canada, continuing to do translations over the internet. Now she is active in the Baha'i community in her new home of Stratford.

Sunday Evenings in the Schoolhouse

Erma Meadows

Outside the window the fields were buried under a thick crust of snow, but the parlour was stuffy and warm. Aunts, uncles, and neighbours filled the small room, talking in muted tones and exchanging solemn glances. Erma, standing unobtrusively in the corner, was too small to see over the edge of the casket which was laid out on the table in the corner. The top of her head only reached to the edge of the dark wood panels.

"Here, I'll lift you up," said the dark-suited undertaker, taking hold of Erma and raising her up so she could see over the edge. A shy five-year-old, Erma was terrified to be lifted up by a stranger. She squirmed and kicked her feet, catching only a glimpse of her father's peaceful face against the satin lining of the casket. Then she broke free from the undertaker's grasp and ran from the room.

Erma Meadows' peaceful childhood on the family homestead near Mannheim was interrupted in 1932, when her family lost the farm due to the financial hardship of the Depression. Only two years old at the time, Erma doesn't have any recollection of the event, but her older brother always remembered moving "from luxury to poverty." The family held a sale, liquidating all the dairy equipment save for a single cow, which they brought with them to their next home, a rented farmhouse. In exchange for free rent, Erma's mother

205

and brothers tended to the beef cattle housed in the barn behind the house. Meanwhile, her father took a job as a hired hand at a farm two miles away. He was away all week, returning only on Sundays to take his wife and young children to church in a horse and buggy.

Misfortune struck another blow to the family three years later. They spent the Christmas of 1936 together happily, but a few days later Erma's father grew ill. For days, he sat by the fire in his rocking chair, pain visible on his face. Although he went to the hospital, doctors weren't able to help him; he died one week later of a ruptured appendix. Erma hadn't known her father well since he lived away from home for most of her life. However, she was aware of the strain that his death placed upon her mother, suddenly a widow with six children and no income.

With no other choice but to carry on, Erma's mother cobbled together a living with all the resources she had at hand. She baked bread and sold it to the neighbours for grocery money and sold cans of cream in town each week to earn an extra $3 to $5. The children would often take a basket of eggs to the store in the morning on their way to school in New Dundee. On the way home, they would pick up the necessary grocery staples: sugar, oatmeal, and sometimes a 25 cent pail of peanut butter. After Easter holidays, Erma's oldest brother dropped out of school and went to work as a hired man. He was disappointed that he couldn't continue on to high school as he had hoped, but he understood that his earnings were desperately needed to support the family.

Erma herself was not particularly fond of school. She preferred the summer months when she would spend long days outside working with her mother in the garden and orchard. She passed many afternoons on the shady back porch, shelling peas, ending beans, and stemming strawberries. Since her mother was busy preserving and baking, the weekly cleaning fell to Erma. Later, the family moved to a house across from the country school, which her mother cleaned in exchange for free rent. Erma and her brother had to carry pails of water for cooking and drinking from the spring behind the barn to their house, which seemed to be nearly a quarter mile away. Each summer, Erma helped her mother scrub down all the desks and oil the floors of the schoolhouse in preparation for the following September.

The schoolhouse had a piano, and the family would often go over on Sunday evenings to sing hymns while Erma accompanied. She had taken piano lessons for one year at their last home, where they had a pump organ. Her father had been musical as well, and she could remember him playing one song on the pump organ with one finger. Erma loved to listen to her brothers' voices blending together in the familiar melodies as she played along with them.

One aspect of school which Erma remembers clearly was the regular health inspections. Students would have to put their hands on top of the desk so their fingernails could be examined. The teacher would also look at their teeth and check to ensure they were carrying a handkerchief. One day when she was in first or second grade, Erma happened to forget her handkerchief at home on the day of the inspection. Fearing punishment, she told the teacher that her handkerchief was in the cloakroom. When she was sent there to retrieve it, she returned empty-handed. For her dishonesty, she was given the strap, a few strikes on either palm. She recalls that it was more embarrassing than painful, but its lesson was long-lasting.

After completing grade nine, Erma was eager to leave school and get to work. She spent two years living with a family who operated a market garden. Twice a week throughout the summer, she would rise at five a.m. to help pack the car with produce and freshly-butchered capons to take to the Galt Market. A few years later, Erma moved to Bridgeport with her mother and took a job at a shirt factory in Kitchener. There, she earned $17 a week—quite an improvement from $6.50 she earned weekly at the market garden.

Several years later, Erma's life took on a new direction. At the time, she was working at the Kitchener hospital as a housekeeper, where she was often in close contact with the nursing students who trained there. "Why don't you go into nurses' training, too?" they would often ask. "You'd get to work with the patients directly." Each time the subject was raised, Erma demurred, protesting that she had never even finished high school. However, the comments continued every couple of weeks, and Erma began to wonder if the Lord was trying to tell her something.

One day after yet another suggestion that she should become a nurse, she decided, "if one more person asks me today, I will consider it a sign from the Lord." Less than an hour later, she was scrubbing the floor when another nursing student offered the familiar suggestion. The realization hit Erma with such force that she was glad she was already on her hands and knees, or she might have fallen over. Still, it took her some time to decide to pursue a nursing career. She did not relish the long stretch of education that would await her, as she assumed she would have to return to grade nine again. Already 25 years old, she worried the other pupils would think she was a grandmother. She was spurred on by the words of a Mennonite evangelist at a tent meeting, and after much prayer, she finally enrolled in high school.

Despite her fears, Erma's experience at school was a positive one. One of the teachers helped her to catch up over the summer, so she could begin in grade eleven. She was far from the only older student in her class—in fact, there were six others like her who were coming back to high school after being out in the workforce. Two years later, Erma returned to Kitchener hospital, this time as a nursing student and then as a full-fledged nurse. She loved her work there, but after a few years, she decided to take a job at a nursing home in

Mitchell that required a registered nurse. When the nursing home changed hands, she applied for a position at Stratford General Hospital and was offered a job the next day.

In 1965, Erma's life took another unexpected turn when she met her future husband, a widower who owned a dairy farm outside of Stratford. She was 36 when she married him and moved out to his farm, caring for his son and father while helping out on the farm. They planted pear, plum, and apple trees to make an orchard like the one at her childhood home. After only 15 years of marriage, her husband fell into the manure spreader while the beaters were going, an accident which placed him in a coma for four months before he died. Erma was left to raise their four children alone. As in all the uncertain times of her life, she trusted in her faith in God to guide her through those difficult years as well.

Erma Meadows.

A Harrowing Journey
Mathilde Watkins

*The girls huddled together on the train plat-
form, looking down the tracks with the sickening
realization that the train was not coming. The
grey packs that they carried with them were heavy,
and they were miles away from the familiar faces
of home.*

*In Stratford and thousands of other towns ac-
ross the world that day, celebrations of VE Day
were in full swing. However, VE day looked much
different in Austria, where Mathilde grew up. The
scene was one of utter confusion. Everyone was
trying to get home to safety, but many were stranded
at the station since the trains weren't running.
There were large groups of soldiers fleeing in trucks,
but with the Russians approaching from the East
and the Americans from the West, nobody knew
which direction to go. Meanwhile, tales of atroc-
ities at the hands of Russian soldiers caused a
growing wave of panic. For a fifteen-year-old girl
simply trying to get home, it seemed to be an impossible journey.*

Mathilde Watkins' fondest memory of her childhood is
singing with her father and four siblings. Her father was a
wonderful yodeller, and he taught his children to sing with
the skill of a choir director. Their voices blended together in
harmony, a bright spot in a very hard life. Her mother and
father both laboured all day simply to earn a little milk and
bread for the family. Mathilde remembers her mother toiling

in the field, while she and her little sister played with the ducks in a creek nearby.

Mathilde is in her father's arms.

Mathilde excelled in school, so she planned to become a teacher. In the Austrian system, students attended teachers' college from when they were age fourteen until nineteen. The school she attended was housed in a former monastery, nestled in the valley town of Sankt Lambrecht. Her days there were happy ones. Though the Second World War was raging and Austria had been annexed by the Nazis, it hardly affected them. They were isolated from the cities without even a radio to bring the news in. She spent her days in the classroom and her free time skiing on the mountains. While she was there, she even competed in ski races.

The end of the war shattered this peaceful existence. One day in May, the teacher came into the classroom and announced that the war was finished. "Anyone who can go home, pack up now. There is a bus waiting to take you to the train station." Mathilde and her friends did not have many belongings to pack. They simply laid out a big grey blanket, placed their shoes, clothes, and books in the centre, and pulled together the ends to make a bag. When the bus dropped them off at the station, they realized that their journey home was going to be more difficult than they had thought.

The trains were cut off at the main station, and it was becoming dangerous to remain there. Disorderly crowds of soldiers, most drunk and scared, were roaming the streets. There were trucks of people continually stopping at the station to see if the trains were running, so Mathilde and her three companions hitched a ride on one of the trucks. They headed down the mountain to another station, hoping to find the trains running there. When they were dropped off there, they were dismayed to find that the situation was no different.

Outside the train station, Mathilde met one of her neighbours from back home sitting on the bench crying. He had been a high-ranking Nazi official, and now he was wondering what was going to happen to him. Most Austrians had opposed the Nazi interference in their country. Now that the regime had been toppled, those who had been German-friendly were no longer welcome in their villages. Away from home so long, Mathilde had known nothing about his involvement with the Nazis.

With no other options, Mathilde and her friends set off on foot, their packs growing heavier with each step. At a crossroads, they were stopped by a soldier and managed to find another ride with a group of soldiers on a truck headed in the direction of their village. Everywhere the air was charged with fear as the Russian army's impending arrival drew nearer. Stories circulated about the theft, rape, and destruction that they left in their wake. The soldiers in the truck were in such a hurry they didn't even stop when they reached Rothentrum, Mathilde's home. She simply had to jump off the back of the truck as it passed.

After six perilous hours, Mathilde was safe in the arms of her parents. Her teenage brother, too, made it home against all odds. He had been drafted into the German army the year before and escaped when the war ended. All alone, he travelled by foot across the mountains to his home. When the Russian army came through their area, they crossed the river right before reaching Mathilde's village, so her family was spared from their terrorism. The men used tubes from the tires of abandoned trucks to transport women across the river, away from the Russians. They were relieved when British soldiers marched into their village.

Mathilde's passport photo.

The hardship did not end with the war, which was followed by great poverty. Inflation made food completely unaffordable, and the black market flourished. For many families, starvation was a real threat; they were truly destitute. Around 1950, Mathilde received a letter from a friend inviting her to come to work in England. She left as soon as she could get a passport. She cleaned house there, as well as in Switzerland. Some places treated her well, and others treated her poorly. It wasn't easy, but she took comfort knowing that if she didn't like it, she could leave. She was hard-working, independant, and resilient.

Eventually, Mathilde decided to fly to Canada, planning to work her way from North Bay all the way down to Brazil. She didn't get nearly that far. Behind the wicket in that northern Ontario train station, she met her future husband. This change of plans brought her eventually to Stratford.

The Chocolate Easter Bunny
Betty Roth

The little girl snuck softly into her aunt's room, careful not to step on the creaky floorboard. She tiptoed up to the dresser, where a beautiful chocolate Easter bunny sat, edged with stiff white icing. Her aunt had received it weeks earlier as an Easter present from her boyfriend, and she hadn't touched it since, preferring to leave it as decoration.

The little girl could not stand by as the delicious chocolate gathered dust on the dresser. She lifted the bunny and carefully broke a piece off the bottom. When she set it back down, it looked exactly as it had before, the layer of icing concealing the missing piece. With a mischievous smile, the little girl slipped the chocolate into her mouth and tiptoed back out of the room.

Betty Roth was born in 1933 and spent her early years in a home on Courtland Avenue in Kitchener. Though her upbringing was in the city, she grew up with a close connection to the farm. On Sunday afternoons, the family would often drive out to Amulree to visit Betty's aunts and uncles on the farm where Betty's mother had been raised. Her father, Ross McGonigle, aspired to be a farmer himself but instead worked as a butter-maker for Silverwood Dairies in Kitchener. The dairy was located right next door to their home, and the horses used for milk delivery were stabled in the lot behind. Betty would often run to the bottom of the hill to reach through the fence and stroke their soft noses.

The Silverwood Dairies' staff photo in 1939.
Betty's father is third from the left in the second row.

When Betty was quite young, she was playing outside in the street when she was run over by a car. She lay flat against the pavement as the car passed directly over her, leaving her without a scratch. She can vividly recall looking up to see the undercarriage of the car above her head. Afterwards, the driver searched the street for her frantically, but she was nowhere to be found. Terrified that she would be scolded for the incident, Betty was hiding under the bed upstairs.

Betty adored school, so much that she would wait every morning at the front door, peering out the window until her primary school teacher came into view on the sidewalk. Then, she would skip down the front steps, and they would walk to school together. Partway through the school year, Betty caught the measles and had to remain quarantined in the house. Each day of her confinement, she stood at the window crying as her teacher passed on her way to class without her.

When Betty was in grade two, the family moved to Wal-

Betty at four.

laceburg where a new dairy was opening up, and then to
nearby Port Lambton the following year. They rented a large
home across the road from the St. Clair River. It was previously the summer home of a wealthy Detroit businessman
who had lost it after the 1929 Stock Market Crash. The river
offered plenty of entertainment for the McGonigle children.
When one of them spotted a large passenger liner approaching, they would announce it throughout the house and hurry
down to the water to swim in the big waves that lapped up
on the shore.

At school in Port Lambton, the primary grades had only
a half-day of school. The younger children, including Betty's
brother Murray, would remain outside in the schoolyard playing after lunch. The boys' favourite game was to swing across
the creek on a rope hanging from a nearby tree. One afternoon, Betty and her classmates were just beginning their afternoon lessons when suddenly a scream from outdoors broke

the studious silence.

Recognizing it as her brother's voice, Betty jumped from her desk—but the teacher strictly reprimanded her, insisting she return to her seat. The school inspector was visiting that day, and the teacher wanted to prove herself as a competent disciplinarian. She took Murray home herself, refusing to allow Betty to come with her. Betty spent that miserable afternoon fidgeting at her desk, beset with worry over her brother's injury. When the afternoon bell rang, she dashed home to hear what had happened. The rope had broken midswing, and he had fallen directly on the concrete culvert, smashing his elbow.

The family had rushed to Chatham hospital, where doctors delivered a bleak prognosis: Murray would likely never regain full movement of his arm. Betty's father refused to accept this so they piled back in the car and headed down the road to the London hospital. There, doctors operated immediately. During his rehabilitation, Murray was placed in a room along with a boy who'd lost his arm in a car accident. His roommate's fate provided Murray with motivation to do his painful exercises. Before long, he was home again, and his elbow eventually healed perfectly.

During summer holidays, Betty and her siblings would often vacation at the farm in North Easthope, where the close-knit family would gather. Betty's aunts loved to dote on her; she can still recall her Aunt Isabel brimming with excitement to give her a brand-new doll that she'd bought for her. One summer afternoon, Betty and her brother were visiting their Uncle Wilmot, a cattle drover who farmed nearby. They were walking in the field when suddenly a team of horses broke loose from the hired man who was harnessing them. The team charged across the field directly towards them, eyes wide and nostrils flaring. Calmly, her tall strong uncle took Murray by one hand and Betty by the other and swung them into the air just as the horses thundered past. They were left

*Betty (left) with her father and siblings
on the front porch of their Port Lambton home.*

dazed but untouched in the dusty air.

While they were living in Port Lambton, the family received a troubling phone call from North Easthope. "Wilmot's been in an accident," Betty's father said when he hung up, hurrying the family into the car. They left before dawn. As she looked out the car window, Betty could see the lanterns on the sugar-beet wagons bobbing in the fields. Throughout the drive, her mother kept repeating, "I can't understand why we're leaving so early. It must be worse than you're telling me." By the time they pulled into the circular driveway of the Avon Crest Hospital, it was daylight, and the whole family was standing outside with sombre faces. Wilmot had been on his way home from a horse race in Forest when the car in which he was a passenger slammed into a culvert. He died soon after from his injuries.

After this tragedy, Betty's mother wanted to be closer to her family, so they moved back to Kitchener. In 1949, the opportunity arose for them to buy the home farm in Amulree. It was a big change for Betty, who left behind a large circle of friends at Kitchener Collegiate Institute. There was a lot of work to be done on their 150 acre farm, especially after her father took on the additional job of township clerk. Betty was often enlisted to help with the paperwork and accounting that the job entailed, figuring out the taxes for the residents of North Easthope Township using a hand-crank adding machine.

When she was 19, she married a local farmer, Edward Roth. Their first home together was an apartment above the store at the main intersection of Shakespeare. The building included a post office and bank which they rented out, as well as a donut shop and general store. Betty ran the store, which was open from eight a.m. until nine p.m, while Edward made the donuts. They quickly settled into a fast-paced morning routine. At four a.m., Eddie rose to start making the donuts. At six, Betty iced and bagged them. By eight, Eddie set off for Stratford to deliver the donuts to local stores while Betty opened the store. The donuts were honey-dipped and made with a secret recipe. They sold for 45 cents a dozen.

With the birth of their daughter, the couple moved to a farm outside of Gadshill where they raised their four children. After the children were grown, Betty and Edward purchased a little cottage on William Street in Stratford. It was an original Ontario cottage which had been built by a labourer in the town's early days, when the focus of the Avon River was work rather than pleasure. They renovated extensively and have lived there, overlooking the Avon, ever since.

References

The following sources were helpful in the writing of this book.

Abella, Irving. *On Strike: Six Key Labour Struggles in Canada 1919-1949.* Toronto: James Lorimer and Company Ltd., 1974. Print.

Bart-Riedstra, Carolynn and Lutzen H. Riedstra. *Stratford: Its Heritage and Its Festival.* Toronto: James Lorimer and Company Ltd., 1999. Print.

Dueck, Peter. *Alternative Service in the Second World War.* Mennonite Heritage Center. n.d. Web.

Elgin County Archives. *No. 1 Technical Training School, St. Thomas.* Elgin County. n.d. Web.

Reid, Barbara R. and Thelma Morrison. *A Star Danced: The Story of How Stratford Started the Stratford Festival.* Toronto: Robert Reid, 1994. Print.

Acknowledgments

First, I would like to extend my gratitude to the individuals who shared their story with me. I was touched by their kindness and generosity.

I would also like to acknowledge the following people who have made important contributions to this book:

John Zupancic and the Conrad Centre for Business, Entrepreneurship, and Technology for the resources and advice which helped to get the project off the ground.

Vanessa DeGroot at Anne Hathaway, Jenna Kelly at the Royal Palisade, Trudy Jonkman at OneCare, and Karen Goforth at Greenwood Court for their assistance in connecting me with interested participants.

Claire Tacon, my creative writing professor and mentor, for her guidance throughout the project and her helpful editorial comments.

My Thursday night Writing Guild—Karla, Elizabeth, Luke, and Stephanie—for being as excited about the project as I was each week. Their enthusiasm and thoughtful comments spurred me on.

My great aunt Joan Scott, for applying her meticulous editing skills to the manuscript.

Jared Windover, for his assistance with the design and formatting of this book. I am grateful not only for his technical expertise but also for the moral support he offered at every step.

Finally, I would like to thank my parents, Debbie Roth and Paul Kroes. Without your encouragement and unfailing belief in my abilities, I never would have had the gumption to take on this project.